AF333741

PSYCHOLOGY
and
RELIGIOUS
EDUCATION

by JOHN L. ELIAS

KRIEGER PUBLISHING COMPANY
MALABAR, FLORIDA

Original Edition 1975
Second Edition 1979
Third Edition 1983, 1990 w/updating

Printed and Published by
ROBERT E. KRIEGER PUBLISHING COMPANY, INC.
KRIEGER DRIVE
MALABAR, FLORIDA 32950

Library of Congress Cataloging-in-Publication Data
Elias, John L., 1933-
    Psychology and religious education / by John L. Elias. -- 3rd ed.,
  updated.
      p.   cm.
  Includes bibliographical references.
  ISBN 0-89464-460-2 (alk. paper)
    1. Religious education--Psychology. 2. Psychology--History--20th
  century. 3. Religious education--Psychology. 4. Psychology-
-History--20th century. I. Title.
  BL42.E4 1990
  268'.01'9--dc20   90-31999
                                                CIP

TABLE OF CONTENTS

To Eleanor, with love and gratitude
To Rebecca and Rachel,
Our loves and our joys

PREFACE TO THE
UPDATED THIRD EDITION

I never expected fifteen years ago that this introductory book on psychology and religious education would go through several editions. That this book is still alive in the world of rapid turnovers in books is a great source of satisfaction for me. I hope that this edition will continue to fill the need of students and teachers of religious education.

This updated edition includes a number of additions. The final chapter of the book brings the treatment up-to-date by including references to articles and books which have appeared in recent years. This edition also includes an index of principal names and subjects. Some minor corrections have also been made in the earlier chapters.

No matter where I have gone in this country and abroad religious educators, especially graduate students, thank me for the clarity and simplicity of the treatment of the topics in this book. I hope the changes that have been made will enhance the value of this book.

My regret in rereading this book is the lack of inclusive language. At the time when most of the book was written the issue of inclusive language had not been raised.

John Elias, Ed.D.
Professor
Fordham University

VITA

John Elias, Ed.D., is professor of Religion and Education at Fordham University, New York. He is the author of numerous articles and reviews. His published books include: *Conscientization of Deschooling: Freire's and Illich's Proposals for Reshaping Society*, *Philosophical Foundations of Adult Education*, *Foundations and Practice of Adult Religious Education*, *Studies in Theology and Education*, and *Moral Education: Secular and Religious*. Dr. Elias has lectured extensively in the United States and the United Kingdom on topics bearing on the intersection of religion, morality, and education.

CHAPTER I

INTRODUCTION: PSYCHOLOGY AND RELIGIOUS EDUCATION

In the popular mind lingers the false impression that there is a hostility between psychology and religion. Many people have the impression that one of the purposes of psychology is to explain away religious phenomena and reduce all religious knowledge and behavior to psychological and naturalistic categories. These impressions have lingered on despite the long tradition of healthy and positive relationships between psychologists and religionists.

Though some psychologists take a dim view of the religious dimension, many prominent psychologists have asserted the positive advantages of a religious orientation of life. Among these psychologists looking favorably upon religion are some of the most outstanding psychologists of the past century: Carl Jung, Erik Erikson, Rollo May, Erich Fromm and Gordon Allport.

As long as the relationship between psychology and religion was viewed with suspicion, religious educators paid little attention to psychology. In recent years, however, with the increase in the awareness that psychology and religion need not be hostile to each other, religious educators have turned increasingly to psychology for help to better understand the task of religious education. The situation has so changed today that psychology is now viewed as an essential discipline in the formation of religious educators. The development of curricula in religious education also manifests this changed atmosphere.

At the outset of this book it is important to make clear the possible relationships that can exist between psychology and religious education. It is first necessary to explain the various terms in this relationship: religion, psychology, and education. To be sure, these terms vary in definitions. No exhaustive attempt will be made to describe the meaning of these terms in ordinary language. But it is essential to clarify these terms to better understand the psychologists presented here.

Religion

Erik Erikson has described religion in a manner which appeals to many people. Religion, for him,

> elaborates on what one feels profoundly true even though it is not demonstrable. It translates into significant words, images, and codes the exceeding darkness which surrounds man's existence, and the light which pervades it beyond all desert or preoccupation.[1]

This description brings out various characteristics of religion. Religion is an ultimate drive or vision of the individual. It is a conversion from an ordinary world to a sacred world. Religion finds various forms of expression: creeds, myths, rituals, codes. It has its roots in the concrete experiences of an individual.

It is interesting that religion is not defined in terms of a belief in God. This shows that Erikson is aware that there are many religious persons; in fact, there are also a number of world religions, which do not maintain a belief in a personal God. The religious person has certain basic attitudes towards the world and human life. He possesses attitudes of reverence, prayerfulness, adoration, courage, oneness, and wonder. These attitudes may be connected with a belief in God and a hereafter, but they also exist outside these beliefs.

Erikson's definition of religion, good as it is, does not, however, do complete justice to the complex phenomenon of religion. Other scholars such as Ninian Smart have delineated various dimensions of the manifold phenomenon of religion. They speak of the *ritual* dimension of religion; the *mythological,* the *doctrinal,* the *ethical,* the *social,* and the *experiential.*[2] This classification of the religious phenomena brings out what is true about religions. They have rites, myths, doctrines, codes of ethics, social organization, and personal experiences. These dimensions of religion are not separate categories because all types of relationships exist between these categories. The experiential dimension gives rise to myths and doctrines. The ritual is often a celebration of myths and doctrines. The ethical dimension springs from the experiential, the mythological, and the doctrinal.

Thus far, in describing the religious phenomenon, I have emphasized what might be termed the positive content. Alongside this content there is the negative content of religion, ways in which the religious experience of man leads to harmful effects on man and society. These must be indicated in order to present the total picture concerning religion. Religion has been used to reinforce the status quo. It is often appealed to in order to sanction one's own particular views and biases. It is presented as a key to peace of soul, the power of positive thinking. Religion can be made a reason for escape from grappling with serious human problems in human terms. Religious adherence can be a mere consensual religion in which one professes religion's faith but does not live one's life according to the tenets and practices of faith.

It can be said that for the most part psychologists have been a bit more interested in the negative aspects of religion than in the positive. This is true because psychology as a discipline has shown more interest in the unhealthy person than in the healthy. But just as the focus of psychology has shifted in recent years to a concern for the healthy, mature, and self-actuated person, so we can expect to see the religious concerns of psychology shift to the healthy aspects of religion. This will be shown to be true in the cases of a number of psychologists that are treated in this book.

Psychology

Most people have a general idea of what the science of psychology is. It must also be stated that it is difficult to give a definition of psychology that would satisfy all the types of psychologies. For our purposes, we might look upon psychology as the systematic study of human persons with regard to their experiences, behavior, and relationships with others. The purpose of psychology is to discover facts, principles, and generalizations about the person that will bring us to a better understanding of total human experience.

Our description of psychology is more accurately termed *general psychology*. Besides this branch of psychology there are others which will have a bearing on our general topic of psychology and religious education. *Social psychology* studies the meaning of persons and their roles in interpersonal relationships. *Psychology of personality* studies the dynamic motivations of persons as they perceive and strive for their goals. *Abnormal* and *clinical psychology* study ways in which persons deviate from normal behavior and ways in which such persons can be treated.

Besides the division of psychology into various fields of study there is also a division of psychologists into various schools of psychology. These various schools of psychology have been termed forces in psychology. The *First Force* is *behavioristic.* B. F. Skinner is an outstanding representative of this group, which attempts to explain man in terms of his overt behavior. Internal states of man are denied. The concepts of freedom and dignity are viewed as illusory. The *Second Force* is *psychoanalytic* and is best represented by Sigmund Freud and Erik Erikson. This approach concentrates on various psychic energies which develop in man and which must be properly directed and controlled. The *Third Force* in psychology looks to the development of the person as a whole. It is best represented in the works of Rollo May, Carl Rogers, Gordon Allport and Abraham Maslow. The emerging, becoming, and developing person is the major focus of this group. They view the previous two approaches as both narrow and reductionistic because they tend to reduce man to only one part of his total being.

When we look at these three major schools of psychology, it should be apparent that the third group would be the most favorably disposed toward religion. While this is true, the first two schools have also examined religious phenomena and have presented significant analyses that can be of great assistance to the religious educator. In this work we will devote attention to all of these Forces in psychology and look at views which do not neatly fit into this threefold division.

Education

There is a sense in which every activity that man engages in can be called educational or a part of education. The ancient Greeks spoke of the education that a person receives as being both part of the community and in touch with the culture of the community. While this is true, it is also necessary to speak of education in a more narrow or technical sense. Charles Silberman in *Crisis in the Classroom* gives a good starting definition for education. He defines it as "the deliberate or purposeful creation, evocation or transmission of knowledge, abilities, skills, and values."[3]

Education is teaching; it is not indoctrination or preaching. It is not propagandizing or manipulating. Education respects the freedom of the student. It presents as certain truth that which is believed to be truth. It shows the options available and presents differences of opinion if they exist and are significant. Education is concerned with the entire person: mind, body, spirit, and character. It is concerned with both thought and emotions. It is not limited to schooling but is a lifelong process. Education attends to the total experience of the person: his culture, language, family, groups, music, arts, etc. Education has respect for the authority of the past and for the experts of the present. But it is also willing to challenge any authority in the name of truth. True education realizes that progress may entail the painful rejection or modification of past ideas.

In recent years we have come to realize the total context of education. Education has *individual* purposes of enhancing personal life at various levels. But it also has *social* purposes. It provides for the continuity of society and for its change and improvement. All education involves a learning community in which all participate. The future will see more education because of the increasing proportion of free time and the rapidity of change. Education is not now viewed as the prerogative of the young but the necessity of all. The enrichment of human life and the continued health of society demands that persons be committed to a lifelong process of learning.

Religious Education

Much controversy has taken place in recent years among religious educators as to the precise nature of their field of endeavor. This is not the place to delve into these controversies. However, benefit may be derived from looking at some of the conclusions that are emerging from these disputes.

First of all, a distinction should be made between *church* education and *religious* education. The former has as its chief purpose to educate a person for membership in a particular church. The latter attempts to educate a person to a religious view of life. The former usually presents a view of only one religion. The latter presents various religious views and also may present the nonreligious view of life.

Religious education should be *experience based.* Religion is not presented as a series of beliefs or events. The religious experience forms the basis upon which beliefs, events, rites, and codes of morality are founded. Religious education aims at personal understanding, conviction, and commitment. It is not interested in the formation of good habits unless these arise from thoughtful commitment. In the presentation of religious truth, religious educators attempt to match the experience of the students and religious truths to be presented. Religious

7

writings are an attempt to put into writing the religious experience of a people.

Religious education *respects past traditions* which formed religious faith. These traditions are not viewed, however, as an albatross preventing further development. The tradition does not present set answers but the living faith of the community; and it often possesses varying interpretations.

It is believed that religion can be taught with both *objectivity* and *strong conviction.* There is no reason why religious education should not entail passionate commitment and involvement on the teacher's part. These two tasks for the religious educator no doubt will present problems and tensions. But the teacher who respects persons and their freedom will be able to resolve all tensions in favor of the student's freedom and the objectivity that the subject demands.

Religious education must be *deeply human.* It must be rooted in the human, the social, the political, the historic, and the cultural. Religion is concerned with ultimate human concerns that arise out of every area of life. Narrowly defined religion possesses the danger of involving people in only ecclesiastical concerns. True religion is prophetic in addressing itself to everything that concerns the human community. True religion must be concerned with the totality of human experience.

Religious education must have an *adult character or mentality.* The ultimate goal of religious education is mature adult faith. Too long educators have written and spoken of religious educators, and in fact, education itself, as if it were an enterprise for children and adolescents only. Recent years have seen hopeful changes of direction. One sees these changes unfortunately more among writers and speakers than among general practitioners. Psychology can make its greatest contribution in the area of adult faith. Extensive literature on psychology remains to be tapped. This literature is concerned with the aspects and problems of the adult. The literature on the older adult is especially useful to educators who care about the religious concerns and crises that take place in the latter part of life.

Psychology and Religious Education

Psychology can make a contribution to religious education in a number of general areas. These will be considered here in order to present some perspective under which various psychologists will be portrayed for their specific contributions to religious education.[4]

Investigating the *nature of religious experience* is a long tradition in psychology. One of the major tasks of psychology is the classification and analysis of total human experience. Religion forms a part of that experience. A psychologist's view of man's religious experience would appear to be greatly influenced by his view of the world, his conception of man, his view of human knowledge, and the methods that he uses in his investigations. Psychological views depend on these presuppositions.

Some psychologists interpret religious experience in a naturalistic fashion; that is, they speak of religious experience as a merely human experience. For *Freud,* religion is a function of man's wishes and desires, an infantile projection. For *Jung,* religion is rooted in the collective unconscious of man. Religious experience to him is the up-rushing of dynamic energies and symbols. *Fromm* reduces the religious experience to ecstatic love for other persons. *Maslow* identifies religion with man's peak experiences and values. Religion refers to those experiences wherein man transcends his ordinary self. These are some of the views that might be termed naturalistic. Other psychologists that might be placed in this category are William James, Erik Erikson, B.F. Skinner and Gordon Allport.

Other psychologists have approached religious experience by assuming that it is a joint product of God's interaction with man. *Rudolph Otto* considers religious experience, a direct experience of God, as the *mysterium tremendum et fascinans* (a mystery which is both overpowering and yet attractive). Other psychologists who have approached religious experience in the same way are Joseph Nuttin, Anton Boisen, and Paul Pruyser. Joseph Havens in his *Psychology and Religion* presents an interesting conversation among psychologists of both these persuasions.[5] This particular dispute among psychologists will probably never be resolved because in this area we are concerned with the basic orientation and world views of these men.

The religious educator can profit by reflecting on this fundamental difference among psychologists who have attempted to investigate the nature of religious experience. The varying interpretations of religious experience should alert the teacher to the possibility that students will share in these different interpretations. The same event experienced by different persons can be interpreted in different ways. The teacher should be aware that his own interpretation is only that − an interpretation, and it should not be imposed upon the students or presented as the ideal or best interpretation of religious experience. Freedom should be allowed in this area as in other areas of religious education. What one ultimately asks about any religious experience or interpretation is what action, behavior, or attitude does it lead to. One can judge the value of a religious experience by its fruits, as William James so often reiterated in his *Varieties of Religious Experience.*[6]

A second area of psychology of great import is *developmental psychology.* Extensive work has been done in recent years by psychologists in describing and explaining the development of the person from earliest years until the end of life. All aspects of the human person have been explored in this developmental psychology. Jean Piaget has described the *cognitive* development of the person, tracing the various stages that man passes through to reach intellectual maturity. Both Piaget and Lawrence Kohlberg have done extensive investigation into the moral development of the human person. They have described various stages of *moral* reasoning of which a person is capable. Research continues in this area to determine whether these findings will have applications across various cultures. The *emotional* development of the person has been extensively researched by the psychologists of the psychoanalytic school. Freud's research is extensive, but many modern-day psychoanalysts have added to it. Freud's delineation of the early stages of oral, anal, phallic, and latency has been extended by the eight stages Erikson identified. These stages of emotional and personal development will be treated later in this book.

Other psychologists have also attempted to treat the development of the human person. Havighurst speaks of developmental tasks. Allport has done extensive research in the area of *personal* development. He feels that previous efforts have been too exclusively concerned with the parts of man at the expense of the total man. Psychologists, such as Maslow and Rogers, look more to what may be termed *interpersonal development*, believing that the person develops only as he grows in his relationships and encounters with other people. The development of man's will or *volitional development* has received impetus among psychologists since the publication of Rollo May's *Love and Will.*[7]

The religious educator can benefit greatly from a knowledge of developmental psychology. A number of representatives from this approach will be considered in this book. In the past ten years religious educators have given more effort to relating religious education to the varying stages of human development.

Educators in the past attempted to teach ideas at various stages in a person's life when persons were not psychologically ready for the teaching of those particular ideas. Ronald Goldman's research in religious education has shown us the fallacy of teaching too much and too soon.[8] Religious education that does not have the proper relationship between personal development and religious teaching is doomed to fail to provide the education that is needed.

11

A third psychological area of particular interest to religious educators may be loosely termed *human behavior*. Psychologists study human beliefs, values, practices, and behavior. Religious educators are interested in these dimensions of human development. Religious beliefs, values, practices, and behavior are not totally different from the ordinary activities of man. Even if one, however, contends that they are different, the many parallels between the religious and the secular realms will afford instructive material for religious educators to consider.

In the area of *beliefs* there is a great deal for religious educators to ponder. Psychologists have explained the nature of belief; they speak of different belief and disbelief systems. Beliefs are held in various ways. Some hold them in an open system, others in closed systems. The distinction depends on whether or not a person will look at contrary or contradictory beliefs or belief systems. Much research has been done on the formation of beliefs. Piaget and Goldman are leaders in this research. Psychologists have investigated the question of how belief is shaped by personality.

Psychologists have also examined the whole area of *religious practices*. The religious educator can benefit from their conclusions. They have concluded that prayer is by no means a rare phenomenon in our country. The process of joining, attending, and supporting a church or synagogue has been found to have profound implications for a person's religious development. A great deal of research exists on the practices of children and adolescents. Unfortunately, much of the research in this area is more of a sociological than a psychological nature. This indicates that research often tells us little about the deeper meaning that religious practices have on the individual.

Religious educators may find of interest in contemporary psychology the great amount of work in *motivation underlying religious behavior*. Various types of motivation are seen to underlie religious behavior: anger, hatred, aggression, love, vocation, achievement, work, conformity, dependency, acquiescence, guilt, fear, and perception of death. Educators must have a clear perception of the kinds of motivation that involve persons in religious thinking and behavior. Care must be taken to make motivation spring from the person rather than be imposed upon him by others. Some forms of motivation must be viewed as dangerous if they are not properly used. Some forms which would be suitable for adult persons would not be appropriate for younger persons. The educator must be careful not to impose his own system of motivation upon the students.

A fourth and final general area of psychology with which religious educators should be familiar is psychological research on the *teaching-learning process.* This includes both theories of teaching and theories of learning. The social science approach to religious education advocated by Dr. James M. Lee in a number of his books has made strong use of this area of psychological study.[9] Recent issues of the journal *Religious Education* have given more attention to this dimension of religious education.

Psychologists have elaborated on theories of learning. Behaviorists see learning as the modification of a person's behavior. Other psychologists look to forms of insight to explain how a person arrives at new knowledge. These theories are not purely academic since learning theories will determine the concrete way in which a person approaches his educational task.

Theories of learning logically give rise to theories of instruction. For too long, religious education has been viewed almost as another form of preaching. The model thus far has too often been preaching the message and looking for the proper response. Education, however, must be distinguished from preaching. It has different purposes and methods. Various models of instruction have been delineated. The *behaviorist model* sees instruction as the attempt to modify behavior through the manipulation of certain aspects of the environment. The *social relations* model is oriented towards man and his culture and draws on social sources. The *personality development* model emphasizes the process in which a person constructs his own reality and achieves the goal of a fully-functioning person. The *information processing* model of instruction places its emphasis on the capacity of the person to process information.

Psychologists have also contributed to an understanding of the teaching-learning process through their work on motivation, needs, evaluation, readiness and other important aspects of the learning process. The religious educator who sees his task as somewhat similar to that of the secular educator will find much that is useful to him in the work of psychologists who have looked deeply into the entire process of teaching and learning.

Summary

This chapter has defined and described some of the key concepts that will be utilized in this book: religion, psychology, education, and religious education. Various ways have been presented in which psychology can be of interest and service to religious educators. The groundwork has been laid for the treatment of a number of influential psychologists whose work can be most beneficial for religious educators in understanding the varieties of religious experiences and their interpretations, the development of the human person, the nature of human behavior and beliefs, and various aspects of the teaching-learning process.

References

1. Erik Erikson. *Young Man Luther.* New York: Norton, 1958, pp. 21-22.
2. Ninian Smart. *The Religious Experience of Mankind.* New York: Scribner, 1969, pp. 6-12.
3. Charles Silberman. *Crisis in the Classroom.* New York: Random House, 1970, p. 6.
4. Merton Strommen (ed.). *Research on Religious Develop-*

ment. New York: Hawthorn, 1971. This is a most significant collection of research studies on religious experience, development, behavior and attitudes. This entire section is indebted to this work.

5. Joseph Havens. *Psychology and Religion.* Princeton: Nostrand, 1968.

6. William James. *The Varieties of Religious Experience.* New York: Longman, 1902.

7. Rollo May. *Love and Will.* New York: Norton, 1969.

8. See chapter four of this book.

9. James Michael Lee. *The Shape of Religious Experience.* Dayton, Ohio: Pflaum, 1971; *The Focus of Religious Education.* Dayton, Ohio: Pflaum, 1973.

CHAPTER II

B. F. SKINNER: PSYCHOLOGIST OF HUMAN BEHAVIOR

B.F. Skinner has been virtually ignored by religious educators. Strommen's monumental and comprehensive handbook on research in religious development contains no references to the man who has been hailed as the most influential psychologist of our time![1] A search through textbooks and anthologies in religious psychology and religious education came up with no mention of the extensive research by Skinner relating to human behavior.

It is easy to understand the reasons for the little recognition that religious educators have given to the work of B.F. Skinner. His devastating attack on autonomous man who possesses internal states of knowing, willing, dignity, and responsibility eliminates the possibility of dialogue with him over essential religious issues. The atheism which he espouses precludes discussion because it is connected with an extremely anti-humanistic view of man.

Though reasons for ignoring Skinner come readily to mind, the religious educators' almost total lack of interest in his work is remarkable when one considers the amount of interest they have shown in Freud with whom Skinner shares many religious views. Presumably, the fact that Freud admits some kind of inner man makes it more possible to dialogue with him about religion. Also psychoanalysts after Freud, notably Jung, Fromm, and Erikson, have shown more positive attitudes towards religion than did Freud.

In the light of religious educators' total avoidance of Skinner's views, I attempted recently in a graduate seminar in religious education to probe, with a number of students actively involved in religious education, his most recent work, *Beyond Freedom and Dignity*, to see what challenges it presents to religious educators.[2] No attempt was made to refute Skinner on religious, philosophical, or psychological grounds. Such attempts may be necessary, but they may also be futile if one is convinced by the sophisticated reasoning of Charles Taylor's *The Explanation of Behavior*.[3] Rather, Skinner, the psychologist-philosopher was accepted as the serious challenger that he is to the fundamental assumptions that underlie all of religious education.

This behaviorist's concern with the religious phenomenon startles one. Religious examples flow easily from his pen. He gives religious beliefs behaviorist explanations. The control that religion has over the lives of people fascinates him. This latter aspect is, I believe, the chief aspect of religion that interests Skinner: he is fascinated by the control that religion has over the lives of large numbers of men and women. He continually compares his proposed technology of behavior with the forces that religion has for control—the behavior of people.

Religion and the Free Man

The chief burden of *Beyond Freedom and Dignity* is an attack on the doctrine of autonomous man: man who possesses freedom, dignity, and destiny. Any view which asserts that man possesses these attributes or any internal states is held to be unscientific by Skinner. The religious view is singled out as one of these views.

> In political science, *theology,* and economics, behavior is usually regarded as the material from which one infers attitudes, intentions, needs, and so on. For more than twenty-five hundred years close attention has been paid to mental life, but only recently has any effort been made to study human behavior as something more than a mere by-product. . .(p. 10) (Emphasis added)

Religion, for Skinner, emphasizes the two features of autonomous man that he finds most troublesome: freedom and responsibility. Remembering his fundamentalist Presbyterianism he grants that some religions have admitted a certain amount of external control over man, for he notes that "theologians have accepted the fact that man must be pre-destined to do what an omniscient God knows he will do. . ." (p. 17).

Skinner's theological example is interesting. Has the extreme view that man is controlled by divine grace (external to man) influenced his view that man is completely controlled by an environment (external to man)? It is interesting to note the similarity between the view that though man is completely controlled by God's grace, civil society must exercise great control over man, and Skinner's view that though man is totally determined by his environment, every effort must be made to make sure that this environment totally controls man. Skinner is thus found wrestling with the theological problem of grace and free will in his struggle to eliminate autonomous man and replace him with a totally controlling environment. He does not resolve the problem but merely restates it; for he is faced with the obvious problem of explaining how a person determined by his environment can shape a different environment by which he can control the lives of other people more effectively. This is similar to the theological problem how a person, determined by grace, can act freely.

Skinner raises important questions for the religious educator. His total denial of human freedom will have few followers. His great emphasis on the effect of the environment will be severely challenged. Few religious educators are prepared to accept his conclusions that man bears no responsibilities for his acts either for praise or for blame. But many are challenged to reflect upon the conditions that rightly influence human responsibility. The religious educator will shrink from Skinner's conclusion that man is nothing but his behavior, but he will at the same time be forced to rethink the great influence of the biological, the purely physical, on the person's behavior. Skinner's exaltation of biological and physical man will force religious educators to take seriously, perhaps for the first time, the consequences of modern biology and physics. The educators in the seminar referred to above discovered for the first time the far-reaching consequences of the theory of biological evolution and physical causation through their contact with Skinner.

Religion and Fear

Skinner's theory of human behavior is primarily based on the concept of positive reinforcements. This means that the greatest inducement to behavior is the positive reinforcement of an action through praise and rewards. In his early experimentation Skinner worked on the modification of animal behavior through such reinforcements. His principles have been applied to men in various types of programs of behavioral modification. Schools, mental institutions, and corporations have utilized these Skinnerian programs.

It is Skinner's contention that society makes little effective use of positive reinforcements over human behavior preferring the apparently easier path of aversive controls. Religion is guilty of an excessive use of aversive or negative reinforcements.

> In one form or another intentional aversive control is the pattern of most social coordination in ethics, *religion*, government, economics, education, psychotherapy, and family life. (p. 26)

> A person resorts to punishment when he criticizes, ridicules, blames, or physically attacks another in order to *suppress unwanted behavior*, . . .Some religions teach that sinful behavior will be followed by eternal punishments of the most horrible sort. (p. 57) (emphasis added)

Skinner strongly criticizes the tendency of religions to appeal to fear and to punishment. He views punishment as an ineffective means of control, for the punished behavior is most likely to reappear after the punitive actions are withdrawn. (p. 58) He views the concept of an all-seeing God as an effective means of preventing escape from the punisher and his punishment (p. 63). For him the Judaeo-Christian idea of conscience serves to internalize the concept of punishment as controlling the behavior of individuals (p. 63). Skinner admits that there have also been efforts in religions to appeal to God's love rather than to hell fire as a form of control, but he does not see this as a predominant tendency (p. 31).

Skinner's view in this area is obviously utopian. His contention that human society can be maintained without aversive controls needs much proof and testing. Utopian though this view may be, the religious educator has much to reflect upon in pondering Skinner's strictures against religions for their excessive use of aversive controls over the behavior of individuals. The appeal to punishment and fear are deeply imbedded in religious traditions. Skinner comes out of such a tradition. These traditions must be used carefully, making adaptations because of what has been learned about man through the development of modern psychology.

Skinner's alternatives to fear and punishment will no doubt be unacceptable to religious educators. He first eliminates certain ineffective measures: permissiveness, the controller as midwife, guidance, dependence on things (Rousseau), mind changing. He proposes a greater control to eliminate the illusion of freedom and dignity. Skinner contends that man will always be controlled. The problem is to make sure that he is controlled by the right forces, resulting in correct behaviors. Most religious educators do not favor the extreme controls that Skinner advocates. But some are moving in his direction.

Religion and Behavior Modification

Skinner's impact on public education has been most extensive, especially through the adoption of procedures of behavior modification. Token economies have sprung up in many schools. The behavior of children is shaped through rewarding them for desired behavior. Educational goals and objectives are cast in behavioral terms. Philosophical and psychological behaviorism often form the basis for these pedagogical practices.

The impact of behaviorism in pedagogical theory and practice is great indeed. It does have serious opposition. Third Force psychologists like Maslow, May, and especially Rogers, represent an opposing point of view which has attracted the attention of many educators. The work of developmental psychologists like Piaget, Erikson, and Kohlberg is also influential in many circles. A whole group of educators oppose the efforts of behavioral modification as an infringement on human freedom. A number of recent lawsuits exists contending that the rights of students and mentally retarded are jeopardized by such practices.

Behavioral modification has found acceptance among some religious educators. The Religious Education Departments at Notre Dame University and at St. Louis University have espoused the social-science approach to religious education. This approach sees religious instruction as consisting "in facilitating the modification of the learner's behavior along religious lines." Lee contends that

> performance or behavioral outcomes are indispensable to religious instruction because it is only by either directly observing or inferring from these outcomes that one can say with any sort of validity that learners have actually learned what was intended.[4]

Lee also advocates that religion be taught in a laboratory setting in which desired behavior modifications can be more efficiently produced because of the deliberately structured environment.

This approach to religious education is obviously influenced by Skinnerian ideas. But it also attempts to maintain the traditional image of man as a free and responsible person. It appears that this social science approach to religious education attempts to accept certain pedagogical conclusions derivable from behaviorism without committing itself to philosophical behaviorism. It rejects the classical conditioning of Pavlov but appears favorable to the operant conditioning of Skinner.

Lee and others who espouse the social science approach interestingly enough make no references to Skinner's works, though I contend that they are greatly influenced by his particular brand of behaviorism. What this approach must grapple with more extensively is the problem of freedom which adoption of Skinnerian ideas raises. Somehow lost in this approach is the nature of religion as an invitation for man to respond freely. Should the deliberate modification of people's behavior be the essential task of teaching religion? This approach to religious education reveals the same simplistic view of human behavior that Skinner espouses: only total control over environment will produce desirable behavior.

Behaviorism and Religious Beliefs

One of the fascinating aspects of *Beyond Freedom and Dignity* is Skinner's behavioristically determined explanation of various religious beliefs. He has this to say about life after death:

> The Christian notion of life after death may have grown out of the social reinforcement of those who suffer for their religion while still alive. Heaven is portrayed as a collection of positive reinforcers and hell as a collection of negative, although they are contingent upon behavior executed before death. (p. 129)

Skinner views personal survival after death as a metaphorical foreshadowing of the evolutionary concept of survival value.

Skinner gives an interpretation of the doctrine of God along behavioristic lines. God is the symbol of ultimate control. He favors a God-symbol which embraces positive rather than negative reinforcers. He argues against the symbol of God as all-seeing, for this type of God becomes the Ultimate Punisher of man from whom men cannot escape.

Skinner easily redefines the concept of sin in behavioral terms. The effects of punishments are shame, guilt and sin, depending upon whether punishment is administered by parent or by peer, by a government or by a church. Religious organizations decide what actions will be sinful. For Skinner the religious organization is a special form of government under which "good" and "bad" become "pious" and "sinful." (p. 110)

One does not have to accept Skinner's behavioristic demythologizing of basic religious doctrines in order to profit from it. Expressions of doctrinal beliefs can stand some reductionist efforts. The clear, neat language of behaviorism, rather than theological writing, may tell us more how certain concepts function in the behavior of people. The concepts of God, sin, heaven and hell do function in some people's lives in the way in which Skinner describes. A theologian may argue that these are distorted views of these concepts. This is certainly a legitimate view. But Skinner's challenge must be faced in so far as he explains how these doctrines actually affect human behavior. Also, though Skinner does not appeal to the scriptural evidence, there are sufficient indications that the distortions he points out are found in these writings.

Religious educators who present these religious doctrines in a more favorable light should be aware of the enormity of their task. A considerable amount of the controls men experience in our society are negative reinforcements. Religions have traditionally appealed to their members through these same reinforcements. Contemporary religious educators are more inclined to speak of love of God than fear of God. Balancing various aspects of reality appears to be the obvious solution.

The value for the religious educator in reflecting upon Skinner's behavioristic interpretation of religious beliefs comes from focusing his attention upon religious teaching translated into behavior. The teaching of religion is usually satisfied with an intellectual understanding of religious doctrine. Skinner looks only to behavior. Even for those who believe that man is more than his behavior, Skinner at least affords the opportunity for reflecting how behaviors, are related to specific beliefs. He also shows how disparate a person's beliefs can be from his behavior.

Behaviorism and Utopianism

A strong current of utopianism is one similarity between

the thought of Skinner and that of religionists. Skinner describes the world which would result if behavior modification became the dominant educational process in a culture. It would be a world in which

> people live together without quarreling, maintain themselves by producing the food, shelter, and clothing they need, enjoy themselves and contribute to the enjoyment of others in art, music, literature, and games, consume only a reasonable part of the resources of the world and add as little as possible to its pollution, bear no more children than can be raised decently, continue to explore the world around them and discover better ways of dealing with it, and come to know themselves accurately, and therefore manage themselves effectively. (p. 205)

Skinner views this world as a real possibility. He believes that we already possess the technology of human behavior necessary to bring it about.

Skinner's utopian view is most similar to a heaven on earth envisioned by others. He does not believe in the power of God to bring about this kind of world nor in the power of man's freedom to accomplish this great reversal of human fortunes. But he does believe in the power of a totally controlling environment. At this point the crucial weakness of Skinner's total view becomes apparent. Environments must be designed. He presumes that some persons appear on the scene who have insights to shape the environment to bring about the utopian vision. The freedom of these persons would appear to be presumed. Otherwise Skinner is committed to maintain the position of Social Darwinists who waited on evolution to bring about change.

It is interesting to compare the utopian vision of Skinner with the utopian vision of another contemporary educational reformer, Ivan Illich.[5] Illich in his most recent writings presents the vision of a convivial society in which production and consumption are controlled to serve the interests of all men. His view is a deeply religious one in which man assumes voluntary poverty, renounces excess wordly goods, practices sexual continence, and works to establish the kingdom of God on earth. Illich, like Skinner, is a totalist in his efforts to maintain his strong adherence to human freedom. He opposes the behavioral controls advocated by a Skinner. His analysis of social reality is more profound than Skinner's, but his knowledge of human behavior appears rather naive alongside Skinner's extended psychological investigations. Both Illich and Skinner buttress their utopian thinking with apocalyptic visions of a coming catastrophe unless their warnings are heeded. Both have taken up the mantle of the prophet of doom and of hope.

Contact with such utopian thinkers as Skinner (and Illich) can well serve the religious educator. Religious education, especially when conducted within the confines of a denominational setting, can become a narrow enterprise focusing on religious creeds, cults, and codes. The utopian thinker raises the broader questions of the culture. He raises the possibilities of change and development. He relates all aspects of culture to each other. Skinner's view of human culture is not the narrow one that one might be expected of a behavioral psychologist. He applies his principles to all areas of culture: art, literature, religion, government, economics, etc. He makes many comparisons between religious phenomena and institutions and other aspects of human culture. In some ways, his broad view of human culture might well be invigorating to individuals who possess a narrow conception of human culture as it relates to man.

Conclusion

Skinner considers himself respectful of the religious dimension of man's existence, however he contends that it must be considered in developing one's view of man and human culture. Religious educators should not ignore Skinner. He can be read to refute him. But he also can be read as one who represents the scientific and technological culture within which religion is taught. Finally, he can be read for his insights into the nature of religious behavior and the influences of religious institutions on the behavior of man and on the total human culture.

References

1. Strommen, Merton P. (ed.) *Research on Religious Development.* New York: Hawthorn Books, 1971.
2. Skinner, B.F. *Beyond Freedom and Dignity.* New York: Knopf, 1971. Further references to this work will be indicated by page numbers within the text.
3. Taylor, Charles. *The Explanation of Behavior.* New York: Humanities Press, 1964.
4. Lee, James M. *The Shape of Religious Education.* Dayton: Pflaum, 1971, p. 56.
5. Ivan, Illich. *Deschooling Society.* New York: Harper and Row, 1971: *Tools for Conviviality.* New York: Harper and Row, 1973.

CHAPTER III

ERIK ERIKSON: PSYCHOLOGIST OF HUMAN DEVELOPMENT

The first psychoanalyst, Sigmund Freud, did not look favorably upon the religious dimension of man. In his book, *The Future of an Illusion,* he viewed religion as the individual's flight from the frustrations of life to an illusory security of belief in a divine father.[1] Freud admits the great power of religion but he does not consider it a healthy human response. He considered religion an illusion. For him illusions are wishes that man engages in. They are not necessarily false or erroneous. The illusion of religion is a regression to the state of childhood. Just as the child looks to an all powerful father when he confronts difficulties, so the adult person looks to an Almighty Father in the face of his frustrations. Man thus projects a father image of power.

Freud's critique of religion is a strong one. It has influenced many psychoanalysts. It has also become one of the standard criticisms of religious faith. Not all psychoanalysts, however, have been convinced of the truth of Freud's views of religion. They admit that Freud has touched upon some of the abuses of religion. Freud studied abnormal persons, and thus was most sensitive to the abuses of religious faith found in neurotic individuals. Psychoanalysts who have devoted more attention to the study of healthy individuals have come to conclusions different from those of Freud. They view religion as a force for maturity in the life of many adults. Carl Jung and Erik Erikson are examples of psychoanalysts who take this more positive view. This chapter will treat Erikson's insights, but before turning to him, it would be beneficial to look briefly at the psychoanalytic theory of Jung because in some ways Erikson is dependent upon him.

Carl Jung

Carl Jung began his work as a disciple of Freud. In later years, however, he departed from Freud's views, especially those on infant sexuality, and began a different approach to psychoanalysis. With regard to religion, Jung took a more positive view than Freud did. He speaks of religion as being a natural function of man. For Jung, man is naturally religious because he has an inborn need and desire to enter into a relationship at a level beyond the person. Jung sees religion as supplying a satisfying form of expression for deep human needs. The dogmas, creeds, and rituals of religion give man an opportunity to express his deepest and most unconscious needs and desires.

Jung considers religion as a necessary element in man's effort to become whole, or individuated in his terminology. Being whole means reconciling the various sides of one's personality. It means coming to grips with the female element that exists in every male; and vice versa; it means coming to accept the dark or sinful dimension in the life of the individual; it means reconciling the person who we are with the various roles that we have in life, for example, father, worker, neighbor, etc. Individuation is often a painful stage through which a person passes in the second half of his life. It is often apparent after the mid-life crisis. According to Jung this effort for wholeness demands that the person find a new meaning and purpose in life. This, he says, can best be accomplished through giving religious expression to one's needs and desires.

Jung is not a particularly easy person to read. His writings delve deeply into psychology and parapsychology. His thought is not always easy to follow. But familiarity with two key concepts within his thought can be of great assistance to religious educators. His ideas on the role of religion in achieving wholeness in the latter part of life can give some perspective to adult education in the area cf religion. A unifying philosphy of life is what many adults look to as an essential ingredient of their religious life. The adult teacher in religion should be prepared to discuss intelligently the deeper problems of human existence.

A second area where Jung's thought can be fruitful for religious educators is his treatment of the dark side of human life. Religion is concerned with sin, guilt, evil and repentance. Jung makes us see that we are to expect darknesses in the way of thoughts, desires, actions, inclinations, etc. The person should not be destroyed by the realization that these elements exist within himself. The awareness of the dark side of human life is especially important for adolescents who first begin to feel within themselves the stirrings of passions, desires, and intentions.

Ego Psychology of Erik Erikson

Probably the most respected psychologist in this country is the Harvard professor, Erik Erikson. Erikson, more than any American psychologist, has studied what it means to grow up in America and face the variety of tasks that the culture imposes upon the individual. This is one psychoanalyst who has maintained the proper balance between theoretical work and clinical study. His practice has included the study of children, youths, and adults. His major works include *Childhood and Society, Young Man Luther, Insight and Responsibility,* and *Gandhi's Truth.*[2]

Before looking at Erikson's ideas on religion, it would be best to explain briefly what the basic approach of Erikson is with regard to the process of human development. Since he sees religion within this process, it is best to be clear about the process itself.

Erikson describes three interrelating processes that take place within each individual. The first process is the *biological development* of the individual. Here, Erikson assumes the insights and the research of Freud which led to the development of the first four stages of biological development: the oral, the anal, the genital, and the latency stage. In the *oral* stage the sucking and eating instincts are developed. In the *anal* stage there is development in the control of the excretory functions of the person. The *genital* stage witnesses the development of certain conflicts between parent and child termed the Oedipus complex. The *latency* stage, not marked by the development of any particular biological function, is a time of inner development.

Though Erikson begins with the biological and psychological data furnished by Freud, he gives this data his own interpretation. The oral stage becomes the time in which the person faces the conflict between trust and distrust. In the anal stage the growing individual is confronted with the challenge to balance his own autonomy and control with a sense of doubt and shame. The third stage becomes a conflict between initiative and guilt. The fourth stage is reinterpreted as a crisis in which the person must face the challenge of industry and overcome any feeling of inferiority or inadequacy.

In reinterpreting or extending the basic four stages developed by Freud, Erikson obviously moves from the biological development of the person to the *psychological development* of the individual ego. Because of his emphasis on this process of development, Erikson's psychology can be termed ego psychology, the psychology which focuses on the development of the individual's personal identity. Erikson advocates the important idea of personal identities acquired through resolutions of conflicts and crises. He contends that there are certain crises which all individuals experience. Each crisis presents an opportunity for growth and development. Various crises of the person occurring during childhood, adolescence, and adulthood are presented. Besides the crises concerning trust, autonomy, initiative, and industry that have been explained, Erikson adds crises of identity, intimacy, generativity, and integrity, which take place in adolescence and adulthood. I will treat these various crises in the context of the role that religion can play in the resolution of these individual crises.

The third process in which the individual is involved Erikson terms *social organization.* Besides his biological development and the development of the ego, the individual must also establish basic orientations to the world around him. In fact, the person can only develop if he establishes these orientations. Erikson shows in *Childhood and Society* that the processes of socialization through child rearing and education are related to what types of people are needed for the particular economic, political, and social needs of the society in which a person is reared. An individual has not only a personal identity but also a social identity. He is a member of various groups in society and he is formed by the values of these groups.

In discussing the social identity of individuals Erikson utilizes examples from the life of the Sioux Indians and the Yurok Indians. He shows how the child rearing practices of these groups are related to the needs of the community. The type of religion which is found among these two groups is conditioned also by the social, economic, and political needs of these groups. The Sioux Indian lived off buffalo hunting. His life needed to be rigorous and strictly regulated. The religion of the Sioux included solitary self torture in which they sought the guidance of the Great Spirit. Religion emphasized the need for fortitude and bravery. The chief religious rite was the solitary vigil of the Indian far off on the prairies.

Erikson contrasts the life and religion of the Sioux Indians with that of the Yuroks who lived off salmon fishing on the Pacific Coast. This group needed a strong sense of communal organization and identity in order to exist. Communal expression of religion is found in this type of community. The dependence of the group on the power of the creator is emphasized. Religious expression is similar to collective play in which the great themes of fertility and fecundity are dramatized.

Through this example, Erikson indicates that the development of the individual is not only a matter of inner growth. The development of the personal ego is greatly influenced by the type of culture within which a person develops. The religion of the individual is not just his personal making. It does not just come from the inside of the person. Religion is conditioned to a larger degree than we realize by the particular culture in which we live.

Erikson's description of the three processes of development within the individual affords useful insights for the religious educator. At times the religious person tends to minimize the effect of the biological dimension of man.

The psychoanalysts show that this dimension is basic to man. Religion to be meaningful must help persons interpret and make sense of their inner strivings, desires, passions, inclinations and emotions. Complete religious expression allows man to utilize these dimensions in their proper form. Religious education must appeal not only to the person's mind but also to his biological and emotional being. Religious education must utilize the arts of music, painting, architecture, and theater in its appeal to the entire man. Religious feelings are not to be considered a lesser expression of religion than religious thinking.

Erikson's treatment of ego development through the resolutions of the eight crises that he delineates can be a most helpful way for religious educators to give perspective to their world. I will treat these crises later within the context of the religion of childhood, adolescence, and adulthood. Suffice it to say that these crises are easily related to the religious tasks that educators can place before the individual. Each of these crises calls for a solution particular to the individual and demands reflection, prayer, and decision. These crises are opportunities for growth and development.

An awareness of the process of social organization can benefit religious educators and help them realize the individuality of persons. Each person has his own social history and identity. Often we tend to put people into groups or categories. This is true in so far as there are similarities among persons. But each person has created his personal and social identity within the particular culture in which he was reared and the particular type of relationships which he has had. This creates a difficult problem for teachers. It means that serious religious education cannot be mass produced. It must include real relationship between persons.

Teachers need to be aware of their own developing persons if they are to effectively teach others. They must be aware that their own personal and social identities are not to be set up as some kind of model which students are

34

to emulate and copy. Teachers must respect the particular development of each student. There are various types of religious personalities. One person may be of a mystical bent and be interested in personal prayer and religious experience. Another person may be attracted to the cultic or ritual in religion. Another may be impressed by the social activist thrust within religion. Teachers should be aware of what their own major religious thrusts are. They should also be aware that their students may have another thrust. Truly effective teachers are sensitive that the religion class must allow for all types of expressions of religious faith.

Erikson's Description of Religion

Erikson's description of religion has already been mentioned in this book. He states that religion

> elaborates on what one feels profoundly true even though it is not demonstrable, it translates into significant words, images, and codes the exceeding darkness which surrounds man's existence, and the light which pervades it beyond all desert or preoccupations.[3]

Erikson's view of religion is influenced by Jung's conception of religion. For him religion develops under the influence of an inherent desire to return to the mother, to basic trust.

Erikson sees the beginnings of the religious dimension of man similar to the relationship which exists between the child and his mother. Basic trust should characterize this relationship. He sees the religious expressions of adults as retracing their earliest inner experiences and reaching back to the earliest years. This idea will be further developed when I examine the religion of childhood as found in Erikson's writings.

Religion for Erikson is not restricted to a narrow dimension of man's life. In his treatment of Luther's life he shows that all data—events, processes, actions, and personal relations—may have either or both a religious and a secular significance. Erikson sees a religious significance in each crisis a person faces. Though some may prefer to speak of these crises without any particular religious dimension or significance, the point that Erikson makes is that for a religious person like Luther these events must have a deeply religious significance. Erikson fits the fundamental aspects of Luther's religious conversion and pilgrimage into a psychoanalytic framework. He sees Luther achieving inner unity and integrity through his religious development.

I find Erikson's description of religion helpful in understanding the place of religion in the development of the individual. I believe he has some useful insights for religious educators. Erikson's tolerance for the possibility of religious belief without a belief in God has been mentioned in Chapter One. His connection of religion with basic trust is also helpful in understanding the role religion plays in the life of most people. People look to religion for strength. There is no possibility of strength unless one has a basically hopeful and trustful attitude. People look to their religious faith to supply this trust. The Scriptures of all religions place great emphasis on the faith and trust a believer should possess. It is good to see that this emphasis also corresponds to the psychological needs of persons throughout their lives.

Erikson's position that all data of human experience be given a religious interpretation can aid religious educators to see the full dimension of man's religious experience. Often teachers prefer to stick with their prepared lesson and do not allow the students to speak about their concerns. Utilizing Erikson's insight, teachers can come to realize that the student's concerns can also be given a religious interpretation. Through skillful questioning and probing the teacher helps the students to see the deeper significance of their concerns. Students who want to speak about their relationships with their parents, their interpersonal relationships, and the shows which they see, can easily turn to the deeper or ultimate dimension of these issues.

Some weaknesses in Erikson's definition of religion have been indicated in Chapter One. These weaknesses should not blind us to the fact that his definition is an excellent starting point to discuss religion. This definition forces us to keep in focus persons of faith, and the influences that human development has on the elaboration and expression of this faith. My experience has been that explanations of faith and religion that appear in sermons and books lack the force of Erikson's description of religion. Theologically oriented descriptions of religion and faith often bypass the human dimension and transport the person into an unreal world. Religious education needs a sound human and psychological basis for religion. Erikson provides this, I feel, though he is not as specific as some would want him to be in explaining the full dimensions of a particular faith.

The Religion of Childhood

As mentioned above, Erikson sees the origins of religious faith in the infant's very first crisis. An infant needs to feel he *can trust* those around him, especially his parents. Trust has a great deal to do with the child's receiving the proper amount of love and nourishment. The amount of trust at this time depends on the quality of the infant's relationship with his parents.

Erikson sees religion as the institution which safeguards the basic trust persons develop in their earliest years. Trust born of care is the foundation of religious faith. Religions provide persons with the opportunity to express their childlike trust in life and in God. Erikson observes that

> all religions have the periodical childlike surrender to a Provider of fortune and health; some demonstration of man's smallness by reduced posture and humble gesture; the admission in prayers of misdeeds and evil intentions; fervent appeals for unification by divine guidance; the insight that faith must be a common faith with ritual practice.[4]

For Erikson then religious faith enables a person to preserve his basic trust throughout his life. He does not say that this is the only means of doing so. But he clearly states that this is a mode of experience and expression many persons utilize to maintain the sense of trust that is necessary for existence. Trust is a necessary condition for the development of mature religious faith.

The second crisis of childhood is between *autonomy* on the one hand and *shame* and *doubt* on the other. This stage must see the development of will power. Parents must exercise care lest the child's will be broken, and thus shame and doubt ensue. It is *will* that enables a person to act on his own behalf and that of others. The wise parent allows the child to exercise *self* control.

Erikson indicates the role that religion can play in this second stage. Religion can be a force that empowers a person to act, and gives him a reason to exist. The development of autonomy is necessary to develop a mature religious faith; for religious faith demands the strong will to live and to overcome the obstacles of human existence. If the child experiences doubt and shame, he will neither trust his powers, nor be satisfied with the way he is exercising them.

Erikson connects the development of autonomy with the child's relationship to his father and to law. The child must feel his will is important; but because of the will of others, there are things he must do. This is an important problem to resolve, for in later life each religious person, or for that matter every person, must face the conflict between his own faith and will and the will and the law of others. Erikson considers that organized religions offer guidelines persons need to balance their lives between personal decision and adherence to external law.

The third crisis, *initiative* versus *guilt,* Erikson associates with man's will to phantasy, play, games and early work. It is also concerned with the development of imagination and conscience. Freud has given this stage a heavily sexual coloring: the chief problem being the resolution of the

Oedipus Complex. By this Freud meant that the child must begin to identify with the parent of his own sex. Erikson sees this stage in a broader perspective, though he does not ignore what Freud has to say about it.

The religious significance of this stage of development should be obvious to a religious educator. Erikson does not develop this significance in any systematic manner; but he does indicate where his thoughts lie. Religious imagination of the child is related to the development of the imagination. Great myths and legends develop the child's religious imagination. Liturgical scholars are showing the relationship between play and liturgy. Games with their interplay of free will and determined rules and laws lay the foundation for the child's moral education. Finally, the development of conscience is of great religious significance.

Erikson advises parents that they must respond positively to the self-initiated activities of their children. If freedom is given to children, then the sense of initiative is reinforced. Questions should be answered; fantasy and play activity should not be inhibited. If the child is inhibited in these efforts, the danger is he will generate guilt over his self-initiated activities. The initiative and imaginative spirit of the child are sound bases for mature and enriching human development. This is to say that they are the best foundation for the religious impulse which finds its expression in stories, rituals, and law.

The final stage of childhood Erikson describes is that of *industry* versus *inferiority*. This is the latency stage delineated by Freud. The child is interested in how things are made, how they work, and what they do. He is interested in making things. He becomes interested in the wider society—the school, the church, and the neighborhood. He manifests a sense of industry. If this industry is not encouraged and if he does not succeed, there is a danger that he will develop a sense of inferiority.

Again, as in the previous stage, Erikson does not explicitly relate this stage to the religious life of the individual. The religious significance of this stage can be seen when a person begins to work with others. He develops a sense of community and collaboration in tasks with others. Religious expression is ordinarily a social or communal expression. It thus demands the type of industry or cooperation that is the goal in this stage of development. Also, the religious dimension of man's existence calls for actions and deeds. The fruit of religious life comes in the doing of the will of God, in the love of neighbor. A sense of industry which excludes a sense of inferiority is necessary if the person is to enter into religious activities. This is especially true in demands religions make in the area of social action.

It is the responsibility of parents and religious educators to see that religion is properly integrated into the child's early life. Basic faith, autonomy, initiative, and industry are not qualities that are achieved once and for all. There is a certain period in a person's life which is crucial for the development of these attitudes. But these are lifelong tasks. Those educating children must be constantly involved in giving them the opportunities to strengthen their trust, exercise their autonomy, maintain their initiative, and extend their sense of industry.

In closing this section on the religion of childhood, I should like to quote striking words Erikson addresses to all those concerned with the education of the child:

> The general problem of man's exploitability in childhood, which makes him the victim not only of overt cruelty, but also of all kinds of covert emotional relief, of devious vengefulness, or sensual self-indulgence, and of sly righteousness—all on the part of those on whom he is physically and morally dependent. . . .*The most deadly of all possible sins is the mutilation of the child's spirit;* this undercuts the life principle of trust, without which every human act, may it feel ever so good and seem ever so right, is prone to perversion by destructive forms of conscientiousness. (Emphasis added).[5]

This strong warning by a rather mild man written sixteen years ago might well serve the recently developed movements for children's rights.

The Religion of Youth

Erikson has the most to offer religious educators in the area of the religion of youth. He established the struggle for *identity* as the chief task of youth. His biography of Martin Luther was intended to be an extensive development of the resolution of young Martin's identity crisis and his struggle for intimacy.

Erikson delineated three elements in the identity crisis of modern youth. First, there is the need for *devotion,* the need for some ideology, some world view. The young person needs a cause to which to dedicate himself. The second element in the identity crisis is the need for *repudiation.* The young person must in some way repudiate part of his past existence. This may take the form of rejecting parents, religion, friends, and former ideologies. It seems necessary for the person attempting to form his own particular identity to stand against the identity which his parents have given him. The third element in the crisis is the need for *moratorium.* Young people need a span of time after their childhood, but before their deeds and works count toward a future identity. For Luther, this time was spent in the monastery. Other young people travel or work at something not to be their life's work.

In Erikson's analysis the identity crisis often takes the form of an authority crisis. The young person begins to doubt the value of authorities under which he has lived. He doubts the authority of his father; if he is religious, he may doubt the religious authorities. Often the youth takes on a negative identity; he takes on precisely those values authorities have warned him about. When it comes to religious faith, the youth chooses to face the nothingness of the world rather than submit to a faith that appears to him to be full of pious words.

The religious significance of this stage in human development should be clear to any religious educator. At this time, religion must be presented as a highly personal matter. The young person needs to be involved in personal ideals and values. Some repudiation of religion is to be expected. In the face of this repudiation, educators must relax and yet attempt to retain loving relationships with their students. Young people may not want or need the formal types of religious education provided. Their needs may not be explicitly religious but more social and psychological.

It appears that many young people in our time are returning to religious faith in order to cope with their identity. However, they are often turning to or presented with forms of religious faith that make identity or salvation appear too easy and even instant and magical. Identity is a painful struggle; it is not achieved by magical conversion. It is a process that demands reflection, study, and work. Educators should guard against giving the impression that one religious act, or one weekend, one retreat can establish a person's personal and religious identity.

In Erikson's stages of development youth's second crisis is the struggle between *intimacy* and *isolation*. Young persons are eager to fuse their identities with others. Intimacy is the capacity of persons to attach themselves to others, to affiliations, and to causes. The question of sexuality and human friendship becomes strong.

The other side of intimacy is isolation, the inability to enter into close relationships. Persons may fear the loss of egos or identities if they give themselves to others. They may be too competitive and combative in this relationship with others.

The religious significance of the struggle to achieve enriching intimacy is easily seen. For the religious person sexual love has a sacred character, for it is one of the deepest human experiences. This love is often compared by religious writers to the love God has for man. Intimacy demands both love and fidelity; these virtues are strongly emphasized within the religious traditions. Fidelity demands that a person sustain his loyalties in spite of inevitable contradictions and frustrations. Love entails the free sharing of identities. The capacity for real love begins in adolescence and is based mainly upon the virtues of fidelity and loyalty.

It is unfortunate that today youth have the least contact with the forces of religion. From the research of men like Erikson it would seem that this is precisely when persons need religion most. This is when they make the most crucial decisions, when they arrive at some sense of their own identity; when they choose what may be their life's work; when they enter into an intimate relationship with another person. If persons are not influenced in these decisions by their religious faith, religion may appear useless to them for the rest of their lives. This is a real danger.

Organized religions must explore ways in which to touch the lives of young people facing these crucial decisions. The Sacrament of Confirmation and similar rites could be deferred to this period. Strong religious education programs could be presented to persons about to enter marriage. I have always felt that the churches neglect this crucial time. They are more often involved only in the ritual elements of marriage. They should allot time and resources to the ministry of preparing people for marriage. Religious counseling should also include as an essential element vocation or calling. In this way religion could influence a person's important decisions of life.

The Religion of Adulthood

Erikson's discussion of the religion of adulthood can first of all be associated with the problem of *generativity* versus *self-absorption* which he poses as the middle age crisis. At mid-life the person has the tendency to look beyond himself and see what he has originated in others. He should be more concerned with future generations and with the nature of future society. The crisis of generativity comes when the person, looking over his accomplishments, feels they are meager, and his accomplishments have stagnated.

Erikson states that this problem of generativity versus self-absorption can be resolved through loving care. The religious dimension of life, I feel, can admirably foster this form of care which Erikson views as so important to resolve the middle age crisis. The concerns of the great world religions are broad and universal. The Christian religion proclaims the loving care of all men as its principal commandment. The life of Jesus is an inspiration for many individuals to devote their lives to the care of others. Religious communities are formed to care for others. This is their principal motivating force.

If Erikson is correct in his analysis of the middle age crisis, then it must be said that there is room for improvement among the churches in meeting the needs of their adult members. Educational programs for adults must focus on the problems that face persons in mid-life: alcoholism, suicide, infidelity, career changes, homes without children, and lessening physical powers. Opportunities must be afforded for adult church members to become involved in works of caring for others. Educational programs should involve persons in a broad range of problems other than their own.

Some have interpreted Erikson's generativity in a narrow manner. They seem to think that he views generativity as closely connected with the person's continual interest in the children which he himself has generated. In *Young Man Luther,* however, Erikson states that generativity is also a possibility for the childless person. A proper form of generativity is man's relationship to God and his dedication to a life of charity. I bring this out in order to underline Erikson's thrust which couples his ideas on human development with the spiritual or religious dimension of a person's life.

The final life cycle in Erikson's schema is termed *integrity* versus *despair,* the crisis facing persons in the later

44

years. Persons possess integrity if they can look over past events of their lives with a feeling of satisfaction and actualization. Despair expresses itself when they feel the time left to them is too short and there is no possibility to take any alternative route. Despair is often accompanied by a fear of death and a sense of personal failure for a wasted life.

The religious significance of this final life struggle should be obvious. All religions are concerned with the ultimate meaning of life and with the fact of death. The churches, however, are slowly developing an adequate ministry to the aged. These efforts with the aged, however, must not be devoted solely to provide them with things to do and to open church facilities to senior citizens. Efforts must be made to come to grips with their psychological and religious problems.

The efforts of religious educators must be directed to the development in the aged of a genuine religious wisdom. Wisdom is manifested by a deep concern with the meaning of life in the face of inevitable death. Wise persons realize their connection with the past, with all that *men* have done, with all that *they* have done. They see meaning in the present life, while realizing the meaning and support that they provide for others. Wise persons can look courageously into the future which will entail the closing of the circle of life. In the later years of our life, everything that we are and do is wrapped around ourselves.

The religious teaching on life after death can be consoling to a person's facing inevitable death. The Christian religion sees love as the answer to the mystery of death. This love is made clear in the unity of the individual with God. A unifying love, begun here on earth, is the response of religions to this mystery. Some may not find this religious solution a particularly believable one. No matter what one thinks of the religious response to death, it is clear that it is only through some form of love and unification, with either one's life, nature, work, family and friends that gives a person the power and the strength to face both life and death.

References

1. Sigmund Freud. *The Future of an Illusion.* New York: Doubleday, 1964 edition.
2. Erik Erikson. *Childhood and Society*, New York: Norton, 1950; *Young Man Luther*, New York: Norton, 1958; *Insight and Responsibility*, New York: Norton, 1964; *Identity: Youth and Crisis*, New York: Norton, 1968; *Ghandi's Truth*, New York: Norton, 1969.
3. Erik Erikson. *Young Man Luther*, pp. 20-21.
4. Erik Erikson. *Childhood and Society*, p. 250.
5. *Op. cit.*, p. 70.

CHAPTER IV

RONALD GOLDMAN: PSYCHOLOGIST OF RELIGIOUS UNDERSTANDING

In 1964, Ronald Goldman published his doctoral dissertation, *Religious Thinking From Childhood to Adolescence.*[1] In the ten years that followed the publication of this book, the work of Dr. Goldman greatly influenced religious education. A companion volume to this research study, *Readiness for Religion,*[2] appeared in 1965. In the former work, Goldman described the capacities of pupils to understand the true nature of religious truths. They were six to seventeen years of age from varying backgrounds. In the second work, Goldman presented a new approach to religious education, one that he considered consonant with his research findings. He termed it a *life-centered* approach to religious education. It is designed to foster the natural interests and needs of the students.

That the developmental stages of thinking described by the Swiss psychologist, Jean Piaget, apply in the field of religious thought is the basic thrust of Goldman's research findings. Piaget's research led him to establish five developmental stages in the origin of the individual's thinking ability: pre-operational thinking, a transitional period, concrete thinking, a second transitional period, and abstract thinking. I will explain these stages below in connection with the stages Goldman found in religious thinking.

Some controversy has arisen about Goldman's research findings both in England, where he originally did his research, and in other countries where his findings and conclusions are influencing the development of curricular materials in religious education. In a later section I will mention some of the prevalent criticisms leveled against the Goldman research. Notwithstanding these criticisms, it is apparent that religious education curriculum and methodology have been greatly influenced in the past ten years by Goldman's research.

The Research Study

1. Description of the Research

In his original research, Goldman applied the criteria of Piaget's various stages of thinking to the responses of 200 children and adolescents discussing three Bible stories. His sample was spread over a number of schools in England and over a number of socio-economic classes. The test consisted of a structured interview which lasted for one or two sessions, according to the age of the child. In the first part, the children were asked to explain three pictures: the first, a child entering a church with a man and a woman; the second, a child kneeling and praying at a bedside; and the third, a child looking at a torn Bible. Various questions were asked of each child interviewed. The second part of the test used a tape recording of a simple paraphrase of three biblical stories of Moses at the Burning Bush, the Israelites crossing the Red Sea, and the Temptations of Jesus. The children were questioned about these stories.

After the responses of all the children were recorded, Goldman analyzed them according to the stages that Piaget had discovered in his examination of the thinking processes of children and adolescents. Goldman examined such concepts as God, His nature, His holiness, His power over nature, His relationship with man, divine justice, divine communication, concepts of Jesus, His humanity and power, concepts of miracles, concepts of the Church, concepts of prayer, and concepts of the Bible.

Goldman and two panels comprising more than forty theologians and educational psychologists conversant with Piaget's levels of thinking did the analysis of the responses of the children. The elaborate statistical analysis shows a high correlation between the ages of the children and adolescents and the corresponding levels of thinking Piaget described.

2. Stages of Religious Thinking

One of the major results of Goldman's research reveals that a person passes through various stages in the development of his religious thinking. Though Goldman basically indicated three stages, he also devoted time, as did Piaget, to discussing the transition from one stage to another. An understanding of these three stages can aid the religious educator in understanding the limitations and possibilities of students of religion at various levels.

Stage One. Pre-Religious Thinking. This is the stage of *intuitive religious thinking.* It can include the 7 or 8 year olds. The child has no real insight into a religious view of life. He has neither the experience nor the mental capacity to think in any logical manner about religious ideas. The child often thinks illogically and comes to inconsistent conclusions. The child responds to religious teaching in ways that are largely conditioned by other ideas recently in his mind. Reversibility is impossible for the child at this stage of development. He cannot work back from inconsistency to check on the evidence in light of the conclusions he has reached.

Goldman gave a number of examples of this type of thinking. One child, when asked why Moses was afraid to look at God, replied that it was because God had a funny face. Another child, when asked the reason why the ground Moses stood on was holy, replied that there was grass on it. Other replies to questions posed to children indicated that they cannot go beyond literal understanding and beyond egocentric concerns. Goldman concluded that these children were incapable of arriving at any religious meaning contained in the stories.

Stage Two. Transition Stage One: Intermediate Stage Between Intuitive and Concrete Religious Thinking. At this stage children strive to break out of the limitations of intuitive thinking. They attempt to produce logical explanations, but they fail because of lack of experience. The child is not capable of concrete operational thinking (to be explained below). The child is not successful in this stage, but the stage is important because the child begins to see the necessity for another process of thinking.

The circular argument in which many children engage is an example of thinking at this level. A child was asked why the ground on which Moses stood was holy. The child states that it was holy because the story said it was. Why? Because God blessed it, replied the child. When the child was asked why God blessed it, he replied, because it was holy. The child is attempting to be logical and systematic, but he is unable to reach to this type of thought. He is in a stage of transition.

Stage Three. Sub-Religious Thinking. This is the stage of concrete operational thinking. It lasts from about 8 to 13 years. Logical thinking is possible at this stage, but only within a restricted area. It is limited to thinking about visible and tangible objects and to the limits of the child's own experience. In this form of thinking religious statements are literally understood. All symbolic statements from the Bible and from other religious sources are interpreted in a literal manner. The child cannot generalize from one concrete incident to another and cannot escape the bounds of his egocentrism. The child will interpret much of what the Bible says about God in an anthropomorphic manner.

Goldman gives a number of examples of this form of thinking. Children view God as a man. The child does not see the symbolic dimension of the story of the Burning Bush. He interprets the story of the dividing of the Red Sea in a literal manner. When asked why Jesus refused to change the stones into bread, a child responded that Jesus had a lot of work to do. Another child replied that he thought that Jesus did not want to show off. These responses show that children at this age were not able to penetrate into the deeper meaning of the religious stories.

Stage Four. Transition Stage Two: Intermediate Stage Between Concrete and Abstract Religious Thinking. At this stage children attempt to do some form of abstract thinking with religious concepts, but previous habits of concrete thinking prevent them from doing so. Children engage in more logical thinking, but they are still distracted by concrete elements of thought. The child at this stage desires to deal with verbal statements and to consider various alternatives or hypotheses. Goldman notes that many persons appear never to advance beyond this transitional stage and thus fail to arrive at a truly religious stage of thinking.

The reply of one child to the question why Moses was afraid to look upon God is an example of this type of thinking. He said that Moses had killed a man. This reply indicates that he was attempting to go outside the story to form an hypothesis. Another child gave this reply to the same question: Moses didn't want to be laughed at by people who wouldn't believe him. One child called the Burning Bush some kind of holy non-burning flame. This child is attempting to go beyond the literal meaning of the story, but he is impeded by looking for some kind of a flame.

Stage Five. Religious Thinking. This is the stage of *abstract operational religious thought.* A child of 13 or 14, begins to be capable of this type of thinking. The child can think hypothetically and deductively. He can think in abstract and symbolic terms. His thinking is consistent because he can see contradictions and try out various hypotheses. He can explore the implications of a statement back to the original argument. Thus he can begin with a theory and work back to facts.

A child at this stage of thinking replied that Moses feared to look upon God because Moses might be frightened of God's greatness. The children saw the Burning Bush as some phenomenon within Moses himself. They gave natural explanations for the miracle of the crossing of the Red Sea. Another child said Jesus would not turn stone into bread because that would be using the power for his own good.

In explaining his developmental stage theory for religious thinking, Goldman notes that religious thinking usually develops later than ordinary thinking. A reason for later development is that religious thinking demands a richer experience before religious language can be used. Religious language is filled with symbols, metaphors, allegories, and parables. Another reason for this later development is the poor or premature teaching given to children which prevents them from developing in the natural sequence of religious thinking. This final reason has led many to examine religious education curricula in the light of Goldman's findings.

3. Research Findings

Goldman provided us with the best summary of his research findings.[3] I can do no better than briefly summarize the findings that he presents in this article.

a. Bible Concepts. The child grasps no real awareness of the nature of the Bible until well into the secondary school. Even at this period, many children regard the Bible as authoritative in a strongly literal sense. Children appear to be unaware of any critical approach to the Bible. All understanding of the children appears to be impeded by a literalism from which even the adolescent finds it difficult to liberate himself.

b. Concepts of God's Nature. Children around the ages of 6 and 7 think of God as a man in crude physical terms. Children around the age of 10 tend to think of God as some sort of a superman with special magical qualities of power and with supernatural signs to symbolize that power. It is only in adolescence that the child overcomes physical interpretations, and God tends to be thought of in less physical terms. Unfortunately, many adolescents, especially those who are disinterested in religion, never get beyond crude anthropomorphic thinking about the nature of God.

c. Concepts of God in the Natural World. Children at an early age tend to equate miracle and magic and see God intervening directly and physically in the natural world. He does this in an arbitrary, spectacular, and artificial manner. Older children begin to form a dualistic world view, one in which God intervenes and the other where scientific laws about cause and effect reign. Even adolescents appear unable to interpenetrate these two separate worlds.

d. Concepts of God's Concern for Men. Younger children deny God's love for all men because they believe

He cannot possibly love naughty persons. Goldman finds that adolescents, however, are capable of understanding the universalism of God's love. Adolescents see the love and justice of God as compatible with God's nature.

e. Concepts of Jesus. Goldman found that until the child was 9 years old, his view of Jesus was extremely confused. Younger children tended to view Jesus as a good man; older children saw him as a magical worker. Only those around the ages of 12 or 14 began to understand the real mission of Jesus. Christ's origins, special status, his function on earth, and their implications are seen only vaguely before mid-adolescence.

f. Concepts of Prayer. Goldman's research found that the young child has a magical view of prayer: prayers will get immediate verbal reassurance from God. Around the age of ten the child moves to a more spiritual appreciation of prayer. But certain magical notions are still included. It is only in adolescence that a more spiritual and realistic attitude is taken towards prayer. Prayer becomes more altruistic and less egocentric. Childish notions of prayer often remain into adolescence and adulthood.

4. *Some Criticisms of the Goldman Research Study*

Goldman's research has greatly influenced the field of religious education. In the latter part of this chapter, I will indicate some of the implications of his research for the educator who wants to be true to the psychological development of the child. In this section I want, however, to indicate briefly some of the criticisms of Goldman's research in order to guide the religious educator into a proper utilization of his research findings. The best appraisal of Goldman's research is found in a symposium printed in the journal *Religious Education.*[4]

Behind Goldman's psychological research lies his *theological presuppositions.* He presumes the biblical view of Rudolph Bultmann and the theological view of Paul Tillich. Thus his approach to the Bible and his approach to theology are decidedly liberal. He accepts the liberal Protestant view that the religious dimension is the deeper dimension of ordinary life. This dimension raises questions about man, justice, morality, love, etc. He also accepts the modern critical view of the Scriptures which sees the meaning of many scriptural passages not in their literal meaning, but in the deeper or symbolic meaning of the written word. Those who do not accept these presuppositions, therefore, will find it difficult to accept many of the conclusions and findings of Goldman's research.

I share Goldman's theological presuppositions. But if I were more conservative or fundamentalistic in my approach to theology, I would be disturbed, for example, by the symbolic interpretations which he presumes as the truth of the Burning Bush incident and the Temptations of Jesus. Much of the criticism against Goldman has been made at this level. Religious educators who look to Goldman for guidance will have to make some decision about their own theological views before deciding on the relevance of many of his findings.

The most serious criticism that I would make of the Goldman research is in his failure to take into account the *affective dimension* of man's being. One cannot fault him for not researching this area, for his research was devoted to religious *understanding*. But when Goldman makes certain suggestions or prescriptions for religious education, this dimension should not be ignored. Because a child cannot articulate an understanding of religious concepts is no reason for stating that religious symbols, words, gestures, stories do not affect him at the emotional or affective level. The area which Goldman has investigated may indeed be an important dimension of religious life, but for many persons conceptual understanding and expression do not have the degree of importance that he seems to give to them.

A third criticism concerns the *choice of stories* he used for the research. The stories he chose would be difficult for the young or even older child to understand properly.

These stories have little connection with the ordinary life
of the child, e.g., the Burning Bush or the Crossing of the
·Red Sea. Goldman would no doubt defend himself by
saying these stories were used in the curricula which he
examined. This may be true, but it is still no reason for
such extraordinary stories being used to ascertain the
religious understanding of children.

My final criticism of the Goldman research is his *failure
to distinguish* between his research findings and his
opinions and suggestions for religious education. This is
not always easy to do, but it is important for a researcher
to keep these two elements safely apart. If the researcher
does not do this, then it appears that the research is the
reason for the opinions and in many cases this is not so.

*Implications of the Goldman Research Study for
Religious Educators*

The implications of Goldman's research for religious
education are found in his highly useful *Readiness for
Religion.*[5] In this work Goldman goes beyond his research
findings and gives the reader his own prescriptions for a
life-centered or a *child-centered* religious education. In this
section of the chapter I will present some of his ideas with
a few observations of my own.

1. The Student

The needs and interests of students should be the first
concern of every religious educator. This sounds like a
cliche, but it is an important principle often neglected in
religious education. Too often religious educators put the
needs of their churches in first place. The religious educator often engages in more or less subtle forms of indoctrination. The needs of the churches for committed members is an important concern, but the needs of students
and their interests come before church concerns. Also, the
needs and interests of students come before the needs and
concerns of their parents. Often parents pressure teachers
·of religion to be too forceful in reinforcing the values of

the parents. This puts teachers in a sensitive area. But it would appear that teachers must not do the bidding of the parents if they view this in any way harmful to the needs and interests of the students.

The first concern of religious educators should be the needs and interests of the students and not the curriculum or content of religious education. Many still think of teaching religion in terms of getting the children and adolescents to learn and memorize facts. Goldman has shown this to be a waste of time in the area of biblical knowledge. Many teachers have had the same experience in teaching doctrine to young children. If Bible or doctrine becomes the first concern of religious education, then religious education will fail to touch students.

It would be well for religious educators to spend a couple of days, if this were possible, following their students through everyday life. If teachers could perceive the experiences, language, concepts, concerns, needs, interests, joys, pleasures, moods, and attitudes of the children they teach, I feel the teaching of religion would be much more in touch with the students' lives. The starting point of religion would then be some concrete happening and not some fact, or event, or statement with which the child cannot easily identify. The starting point in the religious teaching of children is often the things which they see and wonder about. The starting point for adolescents is most often the inner mood, dream, wish, regret, joy, or contentment. Kurt Vonnegut Jr., the novelist, in addressing teachers gave only one bit of advice: *let students speak, listen to them.* I believe this is excellent advice for religious educators. They must listen to the students recount their experiences. Then they can gradually assist them to appreciate the deeper, the spiritual, and the religious meaning of these experiences.

The religious educator should be continuously aware of what Goldman calls the developmental limits in religious growth. I have already indicated the types of immaturity in thinking which Goldman has found through his research: egocentricity, literalism, and concretism in young children. Children also are limited in this use of religious language. They may be able to repeat a symbolic word or phrase; they may even be able to experience it in some emotional manner. But they are not able to understand the symbol, much less able to explain it to others. Finally children have a limited experience upon which to base religious education. They have not lived long; they have limited social experience; their awareness of time and space is limited; their sense of history is undeveloped.

The limitations of children are not a reason for omitting the religious education of the young. They are reasons for carrying it out most carefully and with keen observation of their growth and experience. For example, in speaking to children of the church, an appropriate image would be a family or a group of which they have some experience. It would be better to have children think of God in terms of the things of creation which they directly experience and which reveal the nature and majesty of God.

2. The Aims of Religious Education.

Goldman's life-centered approach to religious education is reflected in his discussion of the aims and goals of religious education. He considers the personal or individual aims of religious education as primary and the social aims as secondary. Individual aims relate to the needs of the students; social aims relate to the needs of churches and of society. For Goldman the primary purpose for teaching religion must be because it is true, because it meets deep human needs, and because without it man's life is indeed impoverished.

Goldman's approach to religious education implies first of all, that religion is not taught primarily in order to inculcate moral values. Instruction in a religious faith that meets the needs of students would be primary. Moral values will spring from this religious faith. The advancement of the Judaeo-Christian culture should not, according to Goldman, be a primary aim of religious education. This

58

approach which is used in religion programs in some public schools in this country is highly intellectual and may not result in any form of religious faith. Thirdly, religion should not be taught for a missionary purpose, to bring members into the Christian or religious community. The danger in this aim, if it is primary, is that the needs of the students might be overlooked in efforts to make Christians out of them.

The basis for religious education in Goldman's *life-centered* approach must be the needs of students. Religion must be presented as a personal search, a personal experience, and a personal challenge. Religion, therefore, must be concerned with the personal needs of students as these are felt at various stages of development. Students must be led to see these needs in depth, which means to understand the spiritual and religious dimensions of their needs. Students have need for love, belonging, trust, acceptance, identity, freedom, positive self-concept, relations to others, understanding, relationship with the divine, and a sense of stability. It is these needs that should form the basis for any *life-centered* or *experience-centered* religious education.

Many teachers immediately respond, in a positive manner, to what Goldman is saying. They have already done this in their classes. Their teaching is truly *life-centered* and *experience-centered.* However, there are other teachers who feel that this program and others like it are not really religious. This type is termed humanistic or secularistic in the sense that it does not appear to deal explicitly with what is usually called religious. How is this different, many ask, from what is done in a good literature course, or social science course, or a humanistically oriented course in the arts?

I do not believe that Goldman's approach adequately responds to this type of objection, though he does attempt to deal with it. Teachers who teach in a *life-centered* or *experience-centered* manner must be versed in the literature, rites, and history of the religious tradition. They must be able to bring this entire tradition to bear upon the life experiences of their students. They must be able to choose out of this entire tradition those elements which are needed by students at particular stages of their development. If students are undergoing identity crisis, teachers must be able to relate this crisis to those elements of the tradition which are concerned with the struggle of persons to achieve their identity.

A teacher, for example, who wants to relate the student's struggle for identity to the religious tradition may use the story of Jesus' baptism, and His trial through the temptations in the desert. The meaning of these events has to do with Jesus' struggle with His proper identity. Many biblical images are utilized in these narratives. Jesus is like Israel of old who must pass through certain temptations in the desert. He is to be the suffering servant of God. His struggle is with the power of evil. He is intimately related to His Father. He gradually comes to a consciousness of His true identity, but only through painful experiences. The identity struggles of other religious figures, Moses, Isaiah and Paul can also be presented as illuminating the present-day struggles of young people.

3. Curriculum of Religious Education

I believe that I have already discussed Goldman's views of the content and methods of religious education in a general way. In discussing the student and the aims of religious education, it is difficult not to pass over what is to be taught to students in religious education. In this section, however, I will give some of Goldman's views relating to children at various stages of their development.

a. Early Childhood (ages 5 to 7). Goldman's research showed that children of this age have no proper religious understanding. Therefore, intellectual data must not be given to children because they will not understand what is being taught or they may learn it in a distorted manner. What is important is the quality of the relationship between teacher and children. It should be loving, warm, sympathetic, and playful. The pre-religious understanding of children is best stimulated through dance, drama, songs and mimicry. Religion should not be taught as a separate subject; there should be no compartmentalization of life. Teachers should be open in pointing out to children the deeper religious significance of their experiences: life and death, the universe, love, sense of belonging, and helping others. The worship of children should be purely spontaneous. They should be involved in the celebration of the great Christian and religious feasts.

b. Middle Childhood (ages 8 to 9). The thinking of children of this age is still concrete, and thus they are not ready to understand the true nature of the Bible. In teaching religion to children, an attempt must be made to avoid identifying religion with the keeping of rules. The teaching of religion must be integrated with life. Some planned religious content can be utilized, but this is best done through various life themes. Themes around which religious ideas can be fostered are home, friends, people who help, pets, shepherds, hands, clothes, mealtime, birthdays, bread, fire, gifts, beginnings and endings. I think it should be clear to religious educators how these themes both touch the lives of students and relate to religious teaching. The life-theme of bread and meals easily lends itself to an introduction to the Last Supper and the Christian Eucharist. From this it is easy to move to some understanding of the Sunday celebration. Children should be actively involved in learning. Goldman gives as an example the making of bread. This can relate to the life theme of bread and then to the deeper spiritual meaning that bread has within the Christian tradition.

c. Late Childhood and Pre-Adolescence (ages 10 to 12). Although the thinking of children at this age is still concrete, they are beginning to move beyond this type of thinking. Goldman recommends that children should be introduced to more critical thinking in order to prepare them for their next stage of development. *Life-themes* teaching should be continued. More biblical material should be introduced. Themes Goldman suggests for use with children of this age include: myself, creation, light, water, sound, growth, air, law and order, names, and stories. Each theme can easily be utilized as an introduction to religious material, and ideas can be drawn from the Bible and the religious tradition. There can be more focus on the person of Jesus. Teaching methods should be active and include looking up material, translating stories into students' experiences, dramatizing the students' interpretations, painting, drawing, diaries, and newspaper reports. Their worship should be connected with real life experiences.

d. Adolescence (13 and older). The adolescent is capable of abstract religious thinking. This does not come about, however, at the same time for all adolescents. Nor do all adolescents reach this particular intellectual potential. Goldman's chief concern with the teaching of religion to adolescents is that they either accept or reject religion for the right reasons and on the right grounds. His studies show that many adolescents stop thinking about religion before they are really capable of serious conceptual thought in religious matters. This is because they are introduced to too many religious concepts which they are not able to properly conceptualize and which have little relationship to their lives. Goldman proposes a serious program of religious education for adolescents, one that attempts to meet their needs. *Life-themes* again make up the program of religious education. These themes include friendship, sex and marriage, snobbery, money, work, leisure, prayer, suffering, learning, and death. Goldman, also, suggests a course on world religions. He emphasizes discussions, role playing and other activities which actively involve students in their own learning as methods of learning.

4. The Teacher of Religion

From Goldman's research and from his recommendations for religious education, it is easy to understand the kind of religion teacher he recommends for the life-centered or experience-centered approach to religious education. Goldman's research concludes that the quality of human relationship between teachers and pupils is the major formative factor in religious education. He maintains that all else stands or falls on this relationship. Teachers are more concerned with their relationships with their students and with the climate of the classroom than they are with the imparting of facts, stories, and events.

Teachers must have a great deal of flexibility. They must be committed to more listening. They must be creative and imaginative in developing activities which lead students to see the deeper, the religious dimension of what they do and experience. Life-centered teachers must ever be learning what are the real life experiences of their children, their hopes and aspirations, their joys and their sadness, their trials and their temptations, their concerns, needs and interests.

I think that I can find no better way to conclude this section and this chapter than by quoting Goldman's insightful words on the proper attitude of teachers when students, whom they have taught, reject religion. I believe that these words contain the basic attitudes that Goldman wants in a religion teacher. He raises the question of whether or not our time with these students will have been wasted.

> It (the time) will have been worthwhile if they grow on into adult life more perceptive, more sensitive and more aware of what life holds for them. They should know, however partially, what it is they cannot accept or have rejected, not because it is confusing, childish, or absurd, but because they have not found it true to their experience, or because having known what it implies they see it asks too much. At least they will understand something of the debt our society owes to the Christian faith, and not least of all they will have savored a human relationship of trust and care, with permissive and

sympathetic adults, in whom this belief is a reality and a power.[6]

References

1. Ronald Goldman. *Religious Thinking From Childhood to Adolescence.* New York: Seabury Press, 1964.
2. Ronald Goldman. *Readiness for Religion.* New York: Seabury Press, 1965.
3. Ronald Goldman. "Researches in Religious Thinking." (In L.B. Brown, Ed.), *Psychology and Religion.* Middlesex, Eng.: Penguin, 1973.
4. *Symposium: Ronald Goldman and Religious Education. Religious Education,* November-December 1968.
5. Ronald Goldman. *Readiness for Religion,* p. 192.
6. *Op. cit.,* p. 192.

CHAPTER V

*LAWRENCE KOHLBERG:
PSYCHOLOGIST
of MORAL DEVELOPMENT
AND EDUCATION*

The seminal research of Jean Piaget has been the inspiration for the work of a number of psychologists. In the last chapter I showed how this research inspired Ronald Goldman to research in the area of religious understanding. In this chapter still another psychologist who has drawn his primary inspiration from the great Swiss psychologist will be considered. Lawrence Kohlberg, Professor of Psychology at Harvard University, has done extensive research in the area of the moral development of the person. From this research he has also presented guidelines for teachers who wish to be involved in the moral education of children and adults. Although Kohlberg does not in his writings forge any connection between moral and religious education, religious educators can find much in his research to aid them in their efforts to present a religiously oriented moral education.

Kohlberg And Piaget

Piaget has done extensive work in the area of the child's moral orientation. His work has been centered on the child's concept of justice and his attitudes toward rules and violations of moral norms.[1] Piaget assumed that there were basically only two levels of moral thought: a childhood level of respect for and obedience to adult authority, and an adult level of regard for others and cooperation with them. The adult level represents a mature level of moral development towards which moral educators should attempt to inspire their students.

The basic thrust of Piaget's concept of moral development is that children develop through interaction with their environment. Development does not take place through the mere maturing of individuals. Nor does it take place because ideas and principles are imposed from the outside. Rather, a two-fold process of assimilation and accommodation takes place. Individuals assimilate the outside environmental experience. But in assimilating it, they put their own stamp upon it because of their own innate capabilities.

66

Kohlberg agrees with Piaget as to the basic process of learning in general, and of moral learning and development in particular. He sees all learning as taking place through the interaction of individuals with their environment. He agrees with Piaget that the center of learning is the active child who structures his or her perceived environment. Kohlberg also agrees with Piaget in postulating various stages of development in moral development and thinking. These stages of development represent the interaction of the child's structuring tendencies and the structural features of the environment.

The fundamental difference between these two psychologists rests, however, in their description of the various stages of moral development. While Piaget assumed two stages of moral development, Kohlberg through extensive interviewing of children was led to hypothesize, not two, but six distinct stages of moral development. Kohlberg also has hypothesized three levels of moral development. Each stage is a different way of perceiving the moral world.

Research Findings

Kohlberg, from his research findings over the past fifteen years, has concluded that moral development is the development of the idea of primitive justice in young children, but becoming more sophisticated as a child passes through distinct stages of moral development. His conclusion is based on his studies of the development of moral values in hundreds of boys, aged nine to twenty-three, in various American communities, in a Taiwanese city, in a Malaysian (Atayal) aboriginal village, in a Turkish city and village, in a Mexican city, and in a Mayan Indian village.[2] These subjects were interviewed about a variety of standard moral conflict situations, and their responses were classified into a system of stages.

Kohlberg's original research in 1958 had been done exclusively with middle-class American boys. In order to determine whether or not these findings were restricted to American youth and to the American system of values, it was necessary for him to test his findings with individuals from highly diverse regions and cultures. These further studies confirmed the various stages which Kohlberg had found in his original research. Kohlberg's original research has also been supplemented by a set of experimental studies, some designed to change the child's stage of moral thought to moral action.

A. Definition of Moral Stages

Kohlberg's most important research findings are the various stages of moral development which he has explained in almost all of his articles on this subject. I will summarize his descriptions of these stages.[3]

I. Preconventional Level

At this level the child responds to various rules of culture as good or bad, right or wrong. He responds to these in terms of various consequences of action: reward and punishment. Kohlberg describes two stages within this first level.

Stage 1. Punishment and Obedience Orientation. The child's main clue to the rightness or wrongness of an action is whether or not he is punished. A child feels that he has done something wrong if he is punished for doing it. Deference to the power of other people is the underlying reason for morality. A child would give this reason for considering stealing as wrong: a person might get caught by the police and then have to spend time in jail. Morality is entirely external; it has nothing to do with intention or desire. The child has no idea that stealing would be wrong if the person were not caught. The child sees the moral relationship between individuals as impersonal and automatic: if someone harms me, I can harm him back. He realizes a primitive sense of justice, an "eye for an eye" 'and "tooth for a tooth" morality.

Stage 2. Naively egoistic orientation. At this stage something is viewed as good because it satisfies one's own needs and occasionally the needs of others. Persons, rules, or actions are the instruments for one's own pleasure. The child has a relativistic approach to values because he can justify whatever he wants to do. Punishment is not viewed as automatic. It rather is due to the whim of the parent or other authority who catches him. The moral world of the child is self-centered. A child at this stage of development will justify mercy killing by asserting that the person would be better off; he would not suffer a great deal.

II. Conventional Level

Within this level of development, conformity to authority becomes significant. Moral value resides in the performing of good or right roles and in maintaining the conventional order and expectations of other people. Persons are interested in maintaining the expectations of family, group, or nation. They have not only a sense of conformity to the social order but also a sense of loyalty to it and to the persons and groups that are involved within it.

It is important to note that Kohlberg observes that it is at this level, and usually among thirteen year olds, that religious conceptualizations begin to merge. Here he echoes the research of Piaget and Goldman. In the earlier stages the child tends to acknowledge vague religious taboos. At this stage there is an idea that one's relationship to God defines one's relations to one's fellow man. One sees here that the Kohlberg research, though done outside explicit religious connections, can offer insights that are beneficial to religious educators. More of this will be indicated in a later part of this chapter.

Stage 3. Good boy, nice girl orientation. That behavior is good which pleases or helps others and is approved by these others. This is the morality of conformity. Children understand rules and see them as helpful. They have naive trust in the authority of parents and of others. Intention now enters into morality. They should be good and nice to others. What parents and authorities approve is assumed to be what should be approved. They earn the approval of others by being nice boys and girls. They see stealing as wrong because it displeases parents, authorities, or God. They see a need to do good to those who do good to them but they see no responsibility to do good to those who harm them.

Stage 4. Law and order orientation. The chief orientation is not for the approval of others; it is rather for authority, fixed rules, and the maintenance of good order in society. "I do right by doing my duty, by showing respect for authority and by keeping things in order." This is the stage of conformity. Persons realize that others have claims on them. People are viewed as earning their rights through hard work. They are unable to distinguish a role from the person who occupies that role. The law and order mentality is characteristic of this stage of development, and the person maintains it is never right to disobey the law. People who break the law must be punished. There can be no justification for civil disobedience. Kohlberg estimates that fewer than one American out of three goes beyond this level of development.

III. Post-Conventional, Autonomous, or Principled Level

At the highest level of moral judgment, moral value resides in the conformity of the person to standards, rights, or duties which he shares with others. Persons define their moral values apart from the authority of groups and persons who hold certain views. They see something as right or wrong, but not in terms of their own identification with the group. They are not able to say: "My country, right or wrong." At this level there is a morality of rights and principles.

Stage 5. Social-contract legalistic orientation. Right action tends to be defined in terms of general individual rights and in terms of standards developed by a society. Kohlberg sees American democracy as founded on Stage 5 thinking. Because personal values and opinions are relative, there must be certain procedural rules for arriving at a consensus among people. The legal point of view is emphasized, as well as the possibility of changing laws by rational considerations. Free agreements and contractual relationships are viewed as binding elements of obligation.

Kohlberg gives as a classic example of this stage of moral development the case of Socrates who suffered death rather than break the laws of Athens. Socrates believed in working to change unjust laws but he did not believe in breaking these laws. His view was that the city could not continue to exist if the legal judgments it pronounced could be destroyed and nullified by private persons. A person might deviate from the law but it would never be right for him to do it. When legal and individual rights come into conflict, individual rights must accede to the majority will as is expressed in the constitutions and laws of the state.

Stage 6. Orientation to universal moral principles. The moral appeal is made to a higher law of conscience or to a divine law which transcends custom and the laws of society. For Kohlberg, the appeal is made to the universal principles of justice, to the reciprocity and equality of human rights, and to the dignity of human beings as individual persons. A person acting at this level wants to be respected, not because he has obeyed the laws of society, but because he has followed the inner dictates of his conscience.

Kohlberg considers the Golden Rule such a universal moral principle. He also considers Martin Luther King's justification for his moral disobedience of the law as an example of Stage 6 thinking. King disobeyed the law out of moral obedience to law and out of respect for justice. He saw that the law was designed to protect the rights of all individuals. King gives this justification for his civil disobedience in his letter from a Birmingham jail:

One has a moral responsibility to disobey unjust laws. . . . I do not advocate evading or defying the law as would our rabid segregationists. That would lead to anarchy. One who breaks an unjust law must do so openly, lovingly, and with a willingness to accept penalty. An individual who breaks a law that conscience tells him is unjust, and willingly accepts the penalty of imprisonment in order to arouse the conscience of the community over its injustice is in reality expressing the highest respect for law.[4]

B. Kohlberg's Conclusions Regarding Moral Stages

Kohlberg contends that this set of stages represents more than just age trends. It is his view that the stages imply *invariant sequences*. Each individual person must go step by step through each of the stages. Persons may go through the various stages at different speeds. They may also become fixated at one particular stage. But if the person moves upward, he must move according to the order of stages that has been outlined.

Stages define *total ways of thinking* in the moral area; they do not represent attitudes toward particular situations. A stage is a way of thinking. Two persons at the same stage of thinking may arrive at different conclusions about a problem. But their type of thinking is the same. For example, two persons at Stage 4 are presented with the question of the morality of stealing a drug in order to save the life of one's wife. One says that you should steal the drug in order to do your duty to your wife. The other replies that you should not steal the drug because this would violate the law. Thus two persons at the same level of moral thinking arrive at different conclusions.

Kohlberg concluded that the stages are *universal*, that is, they apply in all cultural situations. Moral development is not merely a matter of learning the values or rules of a culture, but it reflects something more universal in development. He found the same stages in the various cultures he examined. He also concluded there is no cultural relativity in moral thinking. The same ways or moral valuing are founded in every culture and develop in the same order.

Kohlberg's research led him to *reject the notion that basic moral principles are dependent upon religion.* He found no important differences in the moral thinking of Catholics, Protestants, Jews, Buddhists, Moslems, and atheists. He found religion an important factor in the elaboration of moral themes in different cultures. Religious differences exist with regard to the content of moral beliefs, e.g., views on divorce, eating pork, etc. But the reasoning of religious people to support their views on these matters falls easily into the stages of Kohlberg's research.

A series of studies by Kohlberg and others has indicated that children and adolescents *comprehend all stages below their level, but not more than one level above.* These studies found that the subjects preferred the stage above their own rather than their own stage, or stages beneath. This means that the levels of moral thought limits one's ability to comprehend the moral reasoning of others.

Kohlberg makes clear in his writings that when he speaks of one stage as higher than another, he is making no judgment about the *moral worth* of the individuals at various stages. These stages are levels of moral reasoning and thought, not stages of moral behavior. Assessments of personal worth are not to be made on the reasoning power of individuals. There is no connection between the thought and the behavior of the person. Although Kohlberg's research indicates an awareness of moral behavior by those at higher stages, he admits that this research is not conclusive.

C. Some Criticisms of the Kohlberg Research Findings

Before proceeding to the next part of this chapter wherein I discuss Kohlberg's views of moral education, I want to indicate some of the criticisms that have been leveled against Kohlberg's research. It is good for the religious educator to be aware of these criticisms, lest Kohlberg become the unquestioned authority on moral development and education.

Psychologists criticize Kohlberg on a number of grounds. Those who have used the Kohlberg methods and who have not been thoroughly trained by him have not reached the results that he has. He has been criticized for assuming the invariant sequence without giving adequate evidence that a person goes through the six stages in the order that he proposes. Another criticism psychologists level against him is directed at his claim that his theory has adequate empirical evidence.

Moral philosophers also criticize Kohlberg's stage theory. They find his treatment of justice inadequate because he does not give criteria for determining the deserts of individuals. He emphasizes moral reasoning as the most important element in moral behavior, while many moral philosophers and psychologists contend that the affective and emotional dimension of the person is just as important in determining moral behavior. Many philosophers have asked Kohlberg to more clearly differentiate his stages, because there does not appear to be a clear-cut distinction between the various stages. Many moral philosophers do not accept Kohlberg's Stage 4 as a stage for which people should be educated. A final criticism is leveled at Kohlberg because from his examination of only the area of justice, he concluded with general statements about all of morality. One could also examine a person's progression through various stages of love which might not be related to the types of stages that Kohlberg has found in his examination of justice. A person might progress, for example, from initial dependency to self-assertive love, to mature care, and finally to concern for others.

I do not feel that these criticisms are fatal to Kohlberg's system of moral development. They indicate great difficulty in arriving at truth in this area and the need for constantly revising views and studying evidence. The research begun by Kohlberg continues in his own work and in the work of many of his students. I mention these criticisms in order to bring this lively debate over moral development and education to the attention of religious educators.

In order to understand Kohlberg's views on moral education it is first necessary to look at two approaches of moral education he rejects. His position will become clearer if we look at his reasons for rejecting other systems of moral education.

First of all, Kohlberg rejects the conception of moral education as a determined set of values which teachers impose on students. An example of this form of moral education is the "character education" employed in Russia. Values are determined by bureaucrats, then imposed upon teachers who then impose them upon students. Teachers use the peer groups as agents of moral indoctrination and moral sanctions. They divide the classroom into cooperating groups in competition with one another. If one member of a group does something wrong, the entire group is punished. The group in turn will punish the errant student.

This value education through the imposition of values from the state and the teachers is no doubt an extreme form of education. A lesser form of value education of this type has been described by Richard Dreeben an American sociologist of education.[5] Dreeben argues that demands of classroom management and of the school as a social system unconsciously shapes teachers' activities and performs hidden services in adapting children to society. Through involvement in the social system of the school, students learn to accept the values of the society of which the school is a part.

What Kohlberg finds wrong with both these forms of moral education is that the teachers and schools are engaged in moral education without explicitly and philosophically discussing or formulating its goals and methods. This he considers a rather dubious form of education. Kohlberg believes that both the extreme and the weaker forms of character formation through the hidden curriculum of the school fail to produce the truly moral person who will engage in moral behavior because he is committed to true moral principles. In order to breed loyalty to society and its rules, this form of moral education places loyalty within a school as the highest virtue.

The second approach to moral education which Kohlberg rejects, he terms the "bag of virtues view." Character is formed through exhorting children to practice virtues. Virtues usually presented are honesty, responsibility, service, self-control, friendliness, moral courage, pride, good temper, and generosity. Kohlberg sees Aristotle as the originator of this approach with his four-fold division of virtue into justice, fortitude, temperance, and prudence.

Many virtues were added to this bag of virtues. Kohlberg rejects this approach to moral education for a number of reasons. He appeals to psychological research done by Hartshorne and May who rejected the virtues approach to moral education. They found that the world could not be divided into the honest and the dishonest; almost everyone cheats now and then. If a person cheats in one situation, this does not mean that he will cheat in another. Defining moral aims in terms of virtues and vices is really defining them in terms of the praise and blame a person receives.

In rejecting what he calls the "bag of virtues" approach to moral education, Kohlberg appears to have destroyed a straw man. Many educators have presented a serious and reasoned approach to moral education based on the concept of virtue. One weakness in Kohlberg's approach to moral education, as I shall explain, is that it focuses exclusively on moral reasoning and on the virtue of justice. This approach does not do justice to the full range of human activities nor to the many components that are part of the moral character.

Kohlberg's Program of Moral Education

From Kohlberg's criticism of the programs of character formation and the virtues approach to moral education, he objects to any deliberate efforts to inculcate majority values. Kohlberg follows the ideas of Dewey and Piaget in his program of moral education. He argues that the goal of moral education is the stimulation of the natural development of the individual child's own moral judgment and capacities, thus allowing him to use his own moral judgment to control his behavior. The attractiveness of this approach to moral education is that it allows the person to take the next step in a direction towards which his nature is already directing him; it does not demand imposing another pattern upon him.

In Kohlberg's view, only this indirect approach to moral education respects the autonomy of the person. Any other approach involves some form of indoctrination. The child is free to develop along lines that nature directs him. These lines are the six stages he found through his research.

The first step in moral education in the Kohlberg approach is the Socratic step of creating dissatisfaction in the student about his moral reasoning. Kohlberg does this experimentally by exposing the student to moral conflict situations for which his principles have no ready solution. For example, a small child is asked whether it is right for a person to steal if he is hungry. Another example involves mercy killing or killing in time of war. After the student realizes he has no ready solution to this problem, he is then exposed to disagreement and argument about these situations with his peers. According to Kohlberg's theory the child will understand the reasoning of those who are one step above him. With this conflict situation perceived, the student may then be ready to move to a higher stage of moral reasoning.

Kohlberg has used this method of moral education not only with boys in normal schools but also with boys and men in a reformatory situation. When the experiment began the prisoners were operating primarily at stages one and two. Many of them were able to move to the reasoning found in stage four. In this regard Kohlberg admits that moral reasoning does not necessarily imply moral behavior. But other studies at least point in the direction of some connection between the higher stages of moral reasoning and moral behavior.

Teachers utilizing the Kohlberg approach to moral education act rather indirectly. They do not teach any specific moral content. Rather they are interested in the quality of the students' reasoning. They choose various conflict situations and experiences. Then they expose students to these conflicts and to forms of reasoning higher than their own. What teachers are doing here, according to Kohlberg, is stimulating the natural development of the child along the lines of the six universal stages.

In this form of moral education the teachers must choose real-to-life situations. Real and challenging conflict issues in the moral domain are challenging to children and to adolescents. The situations must be real. The students must realize that there is a conflict here and that the teachers are not playing games. The teachers must be actively involved in the process. It is not the task of the teachers to sneak in their own solution at the end of the discussion and impose them upon the students. The incidents used should not be obvious ones. Children or adolescents will be involved only if they feel that they are engaged in a conflict situation and not some game or school exercise.

Kohlberg and Religious Education

It is my view that the approach to moral education offered by Kohlberg can be a valuable approach to moral education within a religious context. I believe that many religious educators have been using elements of this approach. It also appears to me that certain additions might have to be made to this approach to moral education, if one wants to be true to the religious or Christian tradition within which a person teaches.

Kohlberg's approach to moral education, first of all, *affirms certain values* which are wholly consonant with the Christian tradition. He affirms the value of human *freedom.* His whole approach is an attempt not to indoctrinate the child but to allow and to stimulate him to develop naturally. Kohlberg understands that values imposed upon the child without his rational thought and choice will be values he will easily discard. Secondly, Kohlberg affirms the value of *responsibility*. A person is responsible for the judgments that he makes and the actions that he takes. Praise and blame are found within this system of moral education. Thirdly, Kohlberg affirms the notion of *conscience*. In fact, for Kohlberg the highest stage is reached when the person is most responsive to the dictates of his individual and principled conscience. Finally, in this system of moral education the value of *justice* is given highest priority. Kohlberg considers this sense of justice almost a primitive and innate sentiment which develops as the person moves from one stage of moral reasoning to another.

Kohlberg's approach to moral education can be recommended to religious educators because it places emphasis not on a set of laws but on *rights and relationships.* Christian education has in recent years attempted to move from an approach to morality and moral education which was too centered on a legalistic mentality. The effort in the Kohlberg program is to stimulate the person to move upwards on the scale beyond the law and order approach to the stages wherein rights and conscience are paramount. I believe that his case study approach is well suited to do this, for it affords the person the opportunity to confront moral reasoning at a higher level than his own.

While I believe that the Christian moral educator can easily and profitably use the system of moral education Kohlberg proposes, it is my view that a number of additions or different orientations must be added if the approach is to be truly a religious or Christian one. As a religious educator within the Christian tradition, I would place the *primacy on love* and not on justice. I do not see a conflict between these two virtues or sentiments. But within the Christian tradition it is the ascent to love that is emphasized and not the ascent to justice. Tillich expresses the relationship between justice and love in this way:

> Love does not do more than justice demands, but love is the ultimate principle of justice. Love reunites; justice preserves what is to be united. It [justice] is the form in which and through which love performs its work. Justice in its ultimate meaning is creative justice, and creative justice is the form of reuniting love.[6]

As a Christian educator, I would add to the Kohlberg approach the quality of *spiritual motivation.* While Kohlberg has found that there is no real connection between moral development and a religious orientation, I do not think that the religious educator should conclude that ethics should not be given a religious orientation. Kohlberg's research does not indicate that such a religiously oriented moral education is an impossibility. What he has shown is that no such moral education shows up in his research. This may well be an indictment of the way in which moral education has been carried out in the churches. The moral life of the religious person should show that his basic orientation to moral action comes from his spiritual and religious motivation. If in our moral education in the churches we move from a law-oriented moral education to a gospel—or love-oriented moral education, then I feel people will receive inspiration from the religious tradition.

One problem I anticipate a religious educator would have in using Kohlberg's approach to moral education is his demands that students use their own reasoning ability in arriving at moral judgments. The problem arises, for example, in having students discuss the morality of divorce or birth control within a tradition that views these as wrong. What happens if students arrive at conclusions *different from the religious tradition and teaching?* The examples I have given apply more to Catholic moral education but examples can be given from any religious tradition.

Kohlberg, I believe, wants students to be free to question even the most cherished moral teachings of their traditions. I see some dangers here. Part of the danger lies in Kohlberg's poor treatment of the teaching of morality to the young child. He does not consider the influences of families and other influences on the person's moral judgment and action of the person. He looks at moral reasoning as the chief component of moral judgment and behavior. My view would be that young children should be exposed to the moral teachings of their traditions according to the capacities they have to understand these moral teachings.

As children grow into adolescents, they can be given more freedom to exercise their own judgments on these matters. In teaching adolescents, I believe that the religious teacher can be more direct than Kohlberg proposes. I would make clear to the students the moral teachings of the religious tradition or church and lead them in discussions on these teachings. I would make clear to them my own views on these matters. In all of this I would stand before them as a person who has thought deeply about these matters and who has certain moral convictions. I could not totally be the indirect teacher that Kohlberg advocates. I firmly believe that a teacher can be both committed and fair. I believe that he can show his strong convictions without necessarily indoctrinating students into these convictions.

Conclusion

Kohlberg, in my view, presents a great deal of useful material to the religious educator. But religious educators should not depend entirely on his system of moral education. Insights on moral development from other psychological traditions such as the psychoanalytic, the behaviorist, and personalist, also greatly benefit religious educators. But most importantly, Kohlberg must be supplemented at the theological or religious level. His views are not contradictory to religious teachings. But his ideas should be utilized within the religious teachings that place primary emphasis on love and that give importance to the moral formation of the young and of adults through the concrete living of religious faith in communities of faith.

References

1. Jean Piaget. *The Moral Judgment of the Child.* Glencoe, Ill.: Free Press, 1948.
2. Lawrence Kohlberg. "Moral Education in the Schools: A Developmental View," *School Review, 74:* pp. 1-30, 1966.
3. Lawrence Kohlberg. "Stages of Moral Development as a Basis for Moral Education." In C.M. Beck et al., *Moral Education: Interdisciplinary Approaches.* Toronto: University of Toronto, 1971, pp. 86-88.
4. Quoted in Nancy F. and Theodore Sizer (Eds.) *Five Lectures on Moral Education.* Cambridge, Mass. Harvard University Press, 1970, pp. 76-77.
5. Richard Dreeben. *On What is Learned in School.* Cambridge, Mass.: Addison Wesley, 1968.
6. Paul Tillich. *Love, Power, and Justice.* New York: Oxford University Press, 1944, p. 7.

CHAPTER VI

CARL ROGERS: PSYCHOLOGIST OF THE TEACHING-LEARNING PROCESS

Carl Rogers has been for a quarter of a century one of the foremost psychologists in America. In all his writings he presents the broader view of psychology. The traditional American behavioristic approach to psychology he views as too narrow in its approach to psychology and too confining in its approach to man and his neighbor. Rogers considers himself akin in his psychology to Gordon Allport, Abraham Maslow, and Rollo May. He is committed to the scientific method, but he argues that psychology must not look only to the external behavior of man for its data. It should accept the data of man's consciousness to build a complete description of the mind and spirit of man.

Rogers' orientation in psychology is decidedly clinical. In his major work *Client Centered Therapy*[1] he presented his approach to counseling therapy. In recent years he has applied his principles to other human concerns. Rogers has always had an interest in education. He has been a teacher and a therapist. He has given many talks to teachers and has written a number of papers applying his basic psychological ideas to the field of education. These papers have been collected in his highly influential work, *Freedom to Learn.*[2]

In this chapter I will show the great relevance of Carl Rogers' thought to religious education. Many religious educators have been influenced by his views either directly or indirectly. In any course that I have taught to religious educators they have generally responded most favorably to Rogers. They have seen that his ideas and recommendations have a strong bearing on the conduct of religious education. But I must also point out certain weaknesses in Rogers' theories that religious educators should be aware of in applying his theories to religious education.

This chapter will be divided into the following parts: (1) Rogers' view of man and mental health; (2) the aim of education in Rogers' theory of education; (3) his view on the learning process; (4) the role of the teacher in his theory; (5) the encounter group as a means of achieving true educational community. In each section I will point out how Rogers' ideas might be used within the religious education process.

Rogers' View of Man and Mental Health

The religious educator will feel more comfortable with Rogers' view of man than he will with Skinner's behaviorist view of man. Rogers emphasizes man's freedom and autonomy, his power of self-determination, various subjective stages, his uniqueness, his complexity and unpredictability, his personality, will, intention, and purpose. All of these ideas are most consonant with the religious and Christian tradition.

In *Client Centered Therapy* Rogers has presented nineteen formal principles regarding human nature and human behavior. These principles are concerned with the development of the individual's own sense of reality, with those internal forces which cause him to act, and with the development of the individual's own self-concept. In all of these principles, Rogers presumes the propensity of the individual to grow in a direction that enhances his existence. This growth can be stunted or mistakenly directed unless the proper atmosphere is created and the proper relationships are forged. I will summarize these principles, for they represent Rogers' view of man.

Man is first and foremost a *center of consciousness.* Each individual is the center of a world of his own making. The individual has the power to fashion the world through changes in his internal stages. In other words, reality is the world as I perceive it. My behavior will depend on how I perceive the world. The person does not react to the world in parts but to an organized whole. Rogers considers the person a unity, not an aggregate of parts each of which can act separately.

Self-actualization is the principal tendency of each individual according to Rogers. Through this process the individual attempts to satisfy his various needs. All of man's behavior has purposes which he freely choses. The emotions enter into his decisions but man still remains free even within his emotional drives. Thus for Rogers the best way to understand the person is to understand his internal states as he explains them to others.

Rogers explains the *development of the self* as the gradual differentiation of the self from the entire experience of the individual. As the person interacts with the environment and enters into relationships, he becomes what he is; he becomes a person distinct from all others. The developing self attaches values to certain experiences and sees other experiences as threatening. Some experiences are assimilated into self-concept, others are ignored, still others are given distorted meanings. The tendency of the individual is to assimilate experiences which are consonant with his self-concept.

The individual is *mentally healthy* if he is able to assimilate all experiences into a consistent relationship with his self concept. Any experience which I view as inconsistent with my self concept, I perceive as a threat. In the face of these types of threats, the person does not adjust psychologically. Tensions are produced. Conflicts begin to exist within the person, and he is unable to continue living in any healthy manner.

Rogers' *theory of therapy* is at the heart of his whole approach to man, mental health, and education. To aid a psychologically maladjusted person, one must build helping relationships with him. A cure will take place only if the sick person feels himself to be in an unthreatening situation. The client must become open to his experiences, trust in the wisdom of his self to maintain and enhance itself, be willing to be a process that is ever changing and developing, and while in process be willing to experience ambiguity. Rogers presents certain hypotheses about his therapy: the more a person feels threatened, the more he will exhibit defensive neurotic behaviors; the more the individual is free from threat, the more he will exhibit self-affirming behavior; and he will resolve his anxiety only if he loses the fear of acquiring the trait which threatens him.[3]

According to Rogers the final goal of therapy is the *fully-functioning person.* As shown in this chapter, the fully-functioning person is also the goal of the educational process. This person is able to be each moment what he is capable of being. He is open to his entire being and he trusts it. He functions within a whole range of experiences. He exists as a person in the process of being and becoming himself. This person is open to the entire world of his experiences.

For Rogers, man is primarily a *being in relationship.* Man is defined by his relationships to others. Rogers speaks and writes eloquently and beautifully on the topic of interpersonal relationships. Certain guidelines develop these relationships. Persons must be willing to hear the other person. They want to be heard by that person. They are dissatisfied when they do not hear the other or are not understood. Entering a relationship means the desire to be real or genuine in dealings with others, a desire to communicate this sense of realness to others, and a desire to encounter the deeper reality of others. It entails an acceptance of and a giving of love and a respect for the freedom of others.

Rogers' view of man is obviously romantic and idealistic. It will prove attractive to many religious educators. His view of the person is positive. He beautifully explains the person's potentialities, especially as these relate to relationships with others. From a religious point of view, however, I find two difficulties in totally accepting this point of view. I believe that two safeguards must be added to his general view of man and his capabilities. The religious educator must be concerned with the dark and sinful side of man; he must also be concerned with man's relationship with God.

Rogers does not have much awareness of what the Christian tradition calls *original sin* and what all religious traditions speak of as the sinful nature of man and society. The achievement of virtue and goodness appears too easy. Virtues appear to be a matter of changing one's perspective. The obstacles to achieving the high ideals are nowhere discussed in his writings, nor are the sinful and dark elements within man's being discussed in so far as they impede the development of the fully-functioning man. The harmful social structures which are deterrents and obstacles to full development are not adequately analyzed. It all appears too easy, as if the individual can solve all his problems by merely changing his perspective and perceptions about things. But the reality is that some problems will not go away and man must actively struggle against them.

Religious traditions share many of the ideals which Rogers proposes for man. But I believe many religious persons are more realistic about the difficulties man will encounter in achieving them. In recent years religious thinkers and activists have realized that man's fundamental task is to work for social change, realizing that individual change must proceed hand in hand with efforts to combat many of the social evils weighing down the spirit of man and impeding his full development.

A second corrective that must be applied to Rogers' system if it is to be acceptable to religious education is a treatment of man's *relationship with the Other*. His system is not closed to the possibilities of man's relationship to God as a determining factor in his existence. As far as I know he does not explicitly treat this relationship.

I believe that the best corrective to Rogers' theory of relationships lies in the work of the great Jewish philosopher and theologian, Martin Buber. Buber speaks of a life of dialogue with both man and God. He tells us that God dwells wherever man lets Him in. The earthly mysticism of Buber led him to see that man's relationship with his fellow man is closely related to his relationship with God. His ideas are expressed in these beautiful and important words:

> Creation is not a hurdle on the road to God, it is the road itself. We are created along with one another and directed to a life with one another. Creatures are placed in my way so that I, their fellow creature, by means of them and with them may find the way to God. . . . The

real God lets no shorter line reach him than each man's longest, which is the line embracing the world that is accessible to man.[4]

The religious educator who uses Rogers' ideas on relationships will be well served if he immerses himself in the religious literature that speaks of man's relationship with God. A deepening of this relationship with God will increase the types of relationships that Rogers views as possible among men. The mysterious element of every human relationship will become more apparent as man reflects upon and deepens his relationship to the mystery of being.

The Aim of Education: The Fully-Functioning Person

As was mentioned in the last section, it is Rogers' theory that the goal of education and the goal of therapy are ultimately the same: to produce fully-functioning persons. Rogers from his clinical experience arrived at his concept of fully-functioning persons. His description of these persons is a description of the persons who have successfully come through the therapeutic experience. Rogers sees three facets to this personality.

First of all, the fully-functioning persons are *open to their experience*. They are not persons on the defensive. They are willing to look into everything that they experience. They are open to both the delightful elements of experience and to the painful and sorrowful elements. They do not shut off painful experiences. They have no barriers, no inhibitions that prevent them from experiencing fully what is in their consciousness and in the world about them.

Secondly, fully-functioning persons *live in an existential manner*. Living existentially means that the self and the personality emerge from experience; it means that they realize they are participating in the process of becoming. This type of existence requires a great amount of adaptability, and a changing organization of the self. Persons who live existentially have certain elements of continuity in their existence, but outside these elements they are open to change and flux.

Thirdly, fully-functioning persons *trust their ownselves* in arriving at the most satisfying behavior in each existential moment. If persons are open to their entire experience, they are open to what their memory and their senses tell them and what appears in their imagination. They realize that their conclusions will not be infallible but will be the best possible, given the available data. These persons will be open to the consequences of their actions, and are willing to correct their viewpoints and actions if they realize that they have made a mistake.

Fully-functioning persons are *creative persons.* If persons have the first three attributes, it will follow that they will be creative persons. They will not necessarily be adjusted to the culture. New things can be expected from them, and thus while their behavior is dependable, it will not be completely predictable. In some situations, they will be unhappy. But they will be themselves in all their activities. They will be aware of their inner freedom to fashion the type of persons that they will be.

I believe that with some modifications, the religious educator can utilize Rogers' description of the fully-functioning person as the aim of religious education. As a religious educator, I would also like my students to be open to religious and spiritual experiences. Besides trusting in themselves, I would also like them to realize their limitations and to have a certain degree of suspicion about motivations and actions. Rogers again in this area does not come to grips with the dark side of man's existence.

As a religious educator, I believe that persons cannot usually be thrown on their own resources. They need guidelines, examples, sources of inspiration and motivation offered by the great religious traditions. Rogers appears to believe that the person almost always has within himself the solutions to his problems and the directions within his own potentiality that he should take in life. I am not so sure about this. I believe, at times, people need more direction in therapy and in education than his system seems to provide.

The Learning Process

One of the major features of Rogers' *Freedom to Learn* is his description of the learning process. In this book I have examined the learning theories of Skinner and Piaget. Rogers presents a learning theory that is somewhat akin to that of Piaget and Goldman. But since ·there are certain emphases in this theory not found in the others, it would be useful to examine what Rogers has to say on this point. I believe that religious educators will see some ideas and emphases which may well be introduced into the teaching of religion.

Rogers' theory of learning presumes each person has a *natural propensity for learning*. This propensity can be released under suitable conditions. The chief suitable condition is that the student must perceive the subject matter to have some relevance for his own purposes. He must perceive some meaning in the proposed activity. Learning will take place with great rapidity once the student sees the relevance of the material to be studied or the activity to be engaged in.

An important condition for learning is an *unthreatening atmosphere.* A person will resist some learning if he feels it will demand change in self organization. If external threats are minimal, a person is likely to perceive and assimilate something that threatens him. If the person feels security and love, then he will assimilate some learning which makes strong demands on him.

Rogers is a strong advocate of *learning by doing.* The student must be placed in direct experiential contact with practical, ethical and philosophical, and personal problems.

If the student participates meaningfully and responsibly in the learning process, learning will take place more rapidly. The student should be encouraged to find his own learning resources, formulate his own problems, decide his own course of action, and live with the consequences of these choices. This self-initiated learning should involve the entire person, both intellectually and emotionally. The student should also be initiated into the process of criticizing and evaluating his work.

In looking over these principles I find that the chief tenet of Rogers' theory of learning is that the individual should have the *freedom to learn how to learn.* The student should see the learning process in school as just beginning. Learning should be synonymous with living and experiencing. Learning is to be viewed as a lifelong process of adaptation and accommodation to the situation of a changing world.

In my view Rogers' theory of learning is most suitable for the task of religious education. It is good for the religious teacher to presume that it is the student's natural instinct to be interested in the religious dimension of life. He should be presented with religious ideas, problems, and experiences which are suitable to his experience. I believe that Ronald Goldman has developed such an approach to religious education. The teacher will enhance learning if he is never far from the actual experiences of the students.

The teaching of religion certainly should take place within a non-threatening atmosphere. Religion makes strong demands on the person. An atmosphere of love and security should, therefore, permeate the religion class which is concerned with the love of God and the love of man. Religion teachers, when teaching in the area of morality, must especially be on guard to avoid any threatening atmosphere which would unduly cast fear and apprehension into the minds of their students.

Learning by doing is a good principle for religious education as well as for all elements of the school curriculum. Religion, for too long, has been taught as a set of facts, a group of stories, a code of laws, or a set of regulations. Student participation in religion is crucial, for religion ultimately is concerned with both understanding and commitment. The responsible freedom that Rogers attempts to inculcate in students by having them actively participate in their own learning can well be a major objective of the religious educator. Students should be encouraged to find their own resources in religious and secular literature. They should be encouraged to formulate their own problems. Responsible freedom should be provided for them so that in the learning process they can make their own choices. Through experience they should understand that they must live with the consequences of their experiences and must be ready to make future changes.

The Role of The Teacher-Facilitator

Carl Rogers has done more than any psychologist or educator to develop and to popularize the concept of the teacher as the facilitator of learning. The task of the teacher is to stimulate the students to learn according to their natural desires. Students learn, but it is the task of the teacher to make this learning easy. In this section I will apply what Rogers says concerning the facilitator of learning to the facilitator of religious learning. Rogers speaks of the qualities which make a teacher a true facilitator of learning. He also offers certain guidelines for the facilitation of learning.

The facilitator's first quality is *realness or genuineness.* Rogers means that the facilitators must be aware of their own positions, both intellectually and emotionally. They should be able to live with their feelings and opinions and be able to communicate these to others. The student must meet the real person, not someone who assumes a certain mask or role for the occasion. The real person is vital, with both doubts and convictions.

Religious educators who possess this quality of realness will actually live the tension of faith. They will understand their beliefs and convictions. They will be secure in revealing their true selves to their students. Of course, this has to be tempered with prudence, especially in the teaching of younger children. In an effort to be real, however, teachers must not burden their students with their own particular doubts and problems. The classroom should not be the place for working out their problems. Rogers' discussion of realness lacks this prudential element. Honesty must be tempered with a strong dose of prudence. The effort to be real must be weighed along with the psychological and social situation of their students. This is not always an easy problem to handle, as many religious educators realize, nor are there any easy solutions. Teachers who are guided foremost by what is best for their students will work for their benefit and will resolve disputes in their favor.

Facilitators of learning should be *prizing, accepting, and trusting persons.* Rogers means that they should prize the learners, prize their feelings, opinions and persons. They should care for the learners, but not in a possessive manner. They should accept the learners as separate persons in their own right. They should view the learners as trustworthy persons. True facilitators realize that students are at times apathetic or hostile towards learning. But notwithstanding this, they still maintain a basic trust and confidence in the students.

Religious educators have important reasons for being prizing, accepting, and trusting persons. The relationship between teachers and students is particularly crucial in the area of religion where deeper understanding and firm commitment are ultimate objectives. Teachers of adolescents and youth, especially, should have these qualities. Religious educators will often encounter criticisms, apathy, and severe questioning. If teachers over-react to this type of behavior on the part of students, students may feel that they are being rejected or considered of little worth. Teachers must make it clear that they accept persons, ideas, and opinions of students. They should also maintain their right to be critical of students' ideas.

According to Rogers, facilitators of learning should possess *empathic understanding.* Rogers means that facilitators should have the ability to understand the students' reactions from the inside. This demands that facilitators are aware of how the process of learning appears to the students. This is a most difficult attitude to acquire because many teachers presuppose that they possess it. One barrier to this type of understanding is that teachers ultimately evaluate the work of the students. Teachers are always looking at what the students do from the standpoint of the teacher-evaluator. The first step towards empathic understanding on the part of teachers must be their willingness to spend more time listening and understanding their students, and not always evaluating and making judgments on the students' learning and achievement.

Empathic understanding is a crucial attribute of the religious facilitator. Religion is a dimension of life that is deeply personal to each individual. I am continually amazed how many different approaches people take towards religion in their individual lives. It is most difficult to take all of these perspectives into consideration. Because of these different perspectives, it at times appears almost impossible to treat religion within a classroom situation. But, like it or not, this appears to be the most practical way to carry out religious education. Therefore, the classroom situation must be supplemented by other types of experiences where teachers may in a more casual and informal manner deal with students. Only if teachers and students communicate with one another about deep religious concerns in an unthreatening atmosphere, can anything like the empathic understanding that Rogers speaks of become a possibility.

It is fortunate that Carl Rogers continues the subject of the qualities of the facilitator after he has discussed the three particular qualities I have described. Rogers also offers *a number of guidelines* for the facilitation of learning helpful to a teacher-facilitator.

The facilitators' first responsibility is to set the *initial mood or climate* of the class or group. Before deciding what they want students to learn, facilitators decide on what the atmosphere within the classroom should be. Facilitators will set the proper atmosphere if they initially show themselves as persons who are trusting and accepting and who will make every effort to understand the students and their feelings.

Facilitators then help to *bring out and clarify the purposes* of both the class as a whole and of the individual students. A class need not have a single unified goal. Individuals may have different goals. But it is important for facilitators to have some idea of the different types of goals of their students. They may also make clear what some of their goals are for the class.

Facilitators should *guide and direct the students to pursue their purposes* in the course. Even though some students may want to be led, facilitators should make it clear to students that they are responsible for their own learning. Facilitators guide the students' learning, but it must be the drives and purposes of the students that are the moving force behind the learning process.

A major task of facilitators is to *organize* and make easily available the widest possible range of resources for learning, such as writing materials, persons, audio-visual aids, trips, etc. They present themselves as flexible resources. They can be counselors, lecturers, advisors, persons with many experiences valuable to the group. They can be available to the group as a whole, or to smaller groups and to individuals.

Facilitators should *accept the ideas and feelings* of the individuals. Too often teachers reject unorthodox ideas and strong feelings of the students, not realizing these are ways in which students establish their individual selves. If facilitators are successful at accepting the ideas and the feelings of the group, they can then become *participant learners,* members of the group, and free to express their views.

Facilitators should attempt to arrive at the point where they are able to present *their own ideas and feelings* without fear of appearing to impose these ideas on the group. In such an atmosphere, they can easily give to students honest feedback. They can react to them as individuals who possess their own ideas and feelings. They should, however, be aware of expressions of deep or strong feelings.

One of the most important guidelines for the facilitators, Rogers believes, is that they endeavor to *recognize and accept their own limitations.* Facilitators must recognize how much freedom they can give to students, how strong their desires are to enter into the world of the students, how comfortable they are to express their deeper feelings and how possible it is for them to view students as near equals. Rogers recommends that facilitators express their awareness of their own limitations. In this way, he believes they can get assistance to overcome them.

Rogers' description of the teacher as facilitator is certainly idealistic. It can be assimilated to Dewey's view of the teacher and to the concept of the teacher involved in an open classroom. The emphasis on freedom, openness, and responsibility is appealing. That the teacher should be on an equal footing with students appears to be ideal.

From my experience as a student, as a teacher, as a supervisor of teachers, and now as a teacher-educator, my admiration of Rogers' approach to teaching lessens. I believe that not all teachers can conduct the type of class that he proposes, nor do I feel that this would be a desirable mode of teaching for all teachers and all students. Rogers has developed his view of teachers from his experience as a counselor. Thus he tends to view teachers too much in the mold of the counselor-client one-to-one relationship. This view of teaching would work well in a tutorial situation, but it becomes more difficult as the class increases in size.

Another problem with this mode of teaching is that it tends to neglect the dimension of teaching as imparting and reinforcing skills and knowledge. It is an exaggeration to say that people can discover everything they need to know on their own with only limited guidance from a teacher-facilitator. My experience has led me to believe that though teaching as instruction has been often abused, it still remains an important part of the teaching-learning process. Discovery and good relationships will not bring a person to the fullness of development in religion or in any other subject. There is room for much explanation through interesting and provocative lectures.

The Rogers approach to teaching suffers because it does not seriously treat the adaptations of this mode of teaching to the various age levels, cultural backgrounds, and subject areas with which the teacher may be involved. What is appropriate to one group is not appropriate to another. It is interesting that in *Freedom to Learn* Rogers gives an example of his own facilitation of learning. He chose a class of graduate students in psychology who were required to have a 3.5 grade point average to enter the class. I can see his particular mode of teaching working well at that level. He can presume on ability and on motivation. This mode of teaching would not work as well in other situations.

My advice to religious educators is to look seriously into Rogers' model of the teacher as facilitator. There is much in this model to recommend. But religious educators should not view this model as an exclusive way to conduct religion classes. I believe there is room on the part of the teacher for more direct activity. Many students look for more guidance than Rogers recommends. The honesty of teachers that Rogers calls for must, I believe, be tempered by a necessary prudence that the age of the students, their degree of maturity, and the teacher's own personality will dictate.

True Educational Community Through Encounter Groups

Carl Rogers is closely identified with encounter groups. Since the 1960's he has written and spoken most extensively on what has become one of the most wide-spread contributions of humanistic psychology, the encounter group, also known as the *T-group* sensitivity training, or laboratory training. The encounter group has been advocated as a means to improve and to facilitate self-learning and interpersonal communication. It has also been hailed as a solution to the impersonalism and alienation of our society.

Rogers strongly recommends the encounter group for the educational setting. He contends that its use will lead to better educational leadership through improved interpersonal relationships. He suggests that persons meet first in small groups and then in larger groups. In the beginning, groups should be made up of the same kind of individuals, for example, teachers *or* administrators. Later groups should be vertically structured, with teachers *and* administrators in the same groups. Rogers sees the encounter group within the educational setting as a means of educational change: changing attitudes toward students, and bringing about more cooperative relationships between students, teachers, and administrators.

I believe that religious educators could profit by participating in encounter group relationships among themselves. Too often the teachers involved scarcely know one another. They are often unaware of how other teachers proceed in classes, what they consider important, and where they place their values in teaching.

In my experience the most successful religious education programs were those in which a close relationship existed among the teachers of religion. This is especially true where volunteers were used. Teachers need to feel that they are part of an enterprise with other people. Unless close working relationships exist among religious educators, it will be impossible for individual teachers to achieve a community sense within their own classes. A chief function of the director of religious education is to establish close and helping relationships among the teachers in the program. These relationships can be established, not only through staff meetings but more importantly, through common worship, prayer, and social gatherings. Students who see their teachers as prayerful individuals, who respect and help each other, will provide them with a living witness of faith that will make effective religious education a reality.

References

1. Carl Rogers. *Client Centered Therapy.* Boston: Houghton Mifflin, 1951.
2. Carl Rogers. *Freedom to Learn.* Columbus, Ohio: Merrill, 1969.
3. Carl Rogers. *Two Divergent Trends,* in Rollo May (ed.) *Existential Psychology.* New York: Random House, 1960, p. 89.
4. Martin Buber. *Between Man and Man.* New York: Macmillan, 1965, p. 144.

CHAPTER VII

GORDON ALLPORT: PSYCHOLOGIST OF MATURE FAITH

The topic of one of the more fruitful classroom discussions I have conducted was on mature and adult faith, with a group of religion teachers. They found the discussion challenging, for it demanded that they take a critical look into themselves. Though the process was painful, the results of the discussion were most interesting and helpful. They found mature faith a stabilizing and unifying force; it was manifested in a sense of security. It showed strength in times of crisis, even courage in the face of death. It was concerned with the meaning of life. It gave value to life by making human activities worthwhile. Mature faith provided an understanding of the experiences of life; it made a person aware of his limitations; it was a source of hope, a community support, a pattern and a reason to struggle.

When I look at the characteristics of mature faith that the students uncovered, I realize that the psychologist who best studied mature faith was the American psychologist, Gordon Allport. While other psychologists spent their time and efforts studying various forms of immaturities and abnormalities, Allport devoted his research and writings to the study of the normal and mature human personality. He was interested in the place of religion in the life pattern of the ordinary individual. He did not ignore the operation of authoritarian and immature religion, but his major focus was directed to the development of normal and mature religious faith.

It is my purpose in this chapter to present some of the major facets of Allport's personality theory. I am particularly interested in those aspects of his theory which are concerned with the mature religious sentiment.[1] Allport can guide religious educators in their task of communicating and implementing the notion and the reality of adult religious faith. Skinner provides a view of religious behavior. Erikson is particularly strong in his treatment of the religion of the young person. Goldman gives insights into the intellectual understanding of religious concepts. Kohlberg treats the sensitive area of moral development. But it is only personalist psychologists like Allport who look at the entire person and attempt to treat in a global manner the unique oneness of the human person. From my own experience in teaching, I find that Allport speaks directly and relevantly to the problems of the adults who attempt to arrive at a more mature understanding and living of their faith.

Personality Theory

Allport takes a totalist view of the human person. Neither heredity nor environment explains what the person is. A person is understood in light of his present pattern of motivation as this motivaton functions in his present environment. In less technical terms, I am what I am now because of the present decisions which I make. These decisions have been influenced by many factors, but it is I who decide the person that I am. I am an ever-changing person. What I am today influences what I will be tomorrow, but tomorrow I might make different choices than I have made today.

Allport points to a number of factors that go to form the person that I am today. I will treat each one of these factors briefly. But what is all important for him is that none of these factors totally explains what the human person is. These are all influences but it is I, the unique person, who shape my own person, given these various influences on me.

The first influence on the human personality is what Allport terms *organic desire*. Desire controls much of human life. Men have basic desires for food, water, and shelter. They also have a desire for human stability through companionship. When desires are not met, a person is driven to fear. Another personality theorist, Abraham Maslow, has spoken of these human desires in terms of basic needs that must be fulfilled.[2] If a person is frustrated in his attempts to satisfy his basic human needs and desires, then he does not have the opportunity for further personality development.

A second influence on the development of the human personality is a person's *temperament.* Allport's treatment

103

of temperament is the classical one. He speaks of persons living close to the areas of pain and melancholy; others have a more sanguine view of life. Allport's treatment can be supplemented by the various types of persons classified by Carl Jung. This Swiss psychologist speaks of the introvert and the extrovert. These basic types can be found among persons oriented toward feeling and thinking, passion and action. From these psychologists it becomes clear that a given temperament will influence the development of the individual personality.

The third influence on the development of personality described by Allport is *psychogenic desires and spiritual values.* These desires are to be distinguished from organic or bodily desires. Each individual has desires of a more spiritual nature. A person seeks after truth, beauty, goodness, holiness, self-expression, power, and personal integrity. These desires and strivings are most determinative in the development of the person. It is true that the person becomes what he values most dearly. It is through the seeking of these higher values that he avoids the narrowness of egotism. These values force him to accept the value of other persons. The seeking of these values opens the way for the cultivation of more specifically religious or spiritual values.

Allport terms the fourth influence on personality development, the *pursuit of meaning.* Man is a *meaning-giving* and a *meaning-discovering* individual. Individuals differ according to the type and amount of meaning which they attempt to discover in their lives. But all persons who exercise their rational powers are faced from time to time with circumstances which force them into asking questions about the meaning of their lives and about the meaning of human existence. The personality is forged in the crucible of these critical moments. There is some relationship between the personality theory of Allport and the life-cycle and crisis theory of Erikson. Erikson views the crucial decisions at these critical moments as determining the developing psycho-social personality. Allport does not emphasize them to the same extent as Erikson, but he does see these critical moments as influential forces in the development of the person.

A final factor that Allport draws attention to in his description of the development of personality is the individual's *response to the surrounding culture.* The culture in which a person lives has strong influences on his development. The culture presents opportunities; it also presents obstacles. Notwithstanding the strong force of culture, it is Allport's opinion that the individual is still free to determine the type of person he will be. Allport believes that many social scientists exaggerate the effect that culture has on a person's personal development, when they effectively explain the person in terms of all the external influences upon him. Allport would appear to have the better of the argument here, at least judging from ordinary experience where different types of persons respond differently to the same types of culture.

From these various factors influencing the development of the human personality, Allport indicated three attributes of a mature personality. First, mature person's possess an *expanding self.* They have an ever-widening number of interests of a psychogenic or spiritual nature. Mature persons are not caught up in the struggle for the basics in life. They are able to occupy themselves with objects and concerns of a broader and deeper nature. There is no narrowness or parochialism in mature persons. There is no time of life when they turn off their interest in learning more about themselves and the world. They are ever expanding in their personal contacts and interests in things and events.

The second attribute of the mature personality is what Allport calls *self-objectification.* Mature persons are able to be reflective and insightful about their own life and activities. They are able to look at themselves and what they have done and put this into perspective with regard to their true abilities and limitations. It is interesting that Allport singles out a developed sense of humor as a key aspect of this attribute. Persons who have a sense of humor about themselves are able to avoid taking themselves too seriously. They manifest the ability to objectify themselves. They show that they are aware of their limitations. They possess the necessary detachment and insight of mature persons.

The final attribute of the mature person that Allport points to is *self-unification* or integration. Mature persons possess some unifying philosophy of life. This does not always have to be complete or even articulated in words. It is this unifying factor in their life that supplies the direction and the coherence that are the necessary ingredients of a mature personality. Without this philosophy, the person's life can appear undirected and fragmented. This attribute of the mature personality bears strong resemblance to the process of individuation found in the personality theory of Carl Jung.

Religion and Personality

Allport's approach to religion, especially in his *The Individual and His Religion,* is purely psychological. He is interested in how religion functions in the life of an individual. He shows little interest in institutionalized forms of religion, except insofar as these affect the individual. Allport is also not interested in the claims of revealed religion, again except as these affect the personal living of religious faith. He is more interested in mature religious faith than in immature or authoritarian expressions of religion. One of his fundamental beliefs is that a person can attain mature religious development with a religious view of life. He is also sensitive to the fact that religion functions as a crutch for the immature person.

Allport's treatment of religion is closely connected with his personality theory. That is the reason why I have discussed this theory at some length. But before I pass to his treatment of the religious sentiment within the developing personality, it is necessary to explain a crucial distinction that Allport makes of religion. Allport distinguishes between intrinsic and extrinsic religion. A person's religious orientation is *extrinsic* if religion is a matter of conformity for a person. It is not basic to the development of the person. A person is *intrinsically* oriented to religion if religion is a formative factor in his development, and if it is a major motivating factor in his life and activities. Allport sees extrinsic and intrinsic along a continuum; it is not a matter of one or the other. He expresses the difference between these two types of religion in this manner: the extrinsically motivated person *uses* his religion, whereas the intrinsically motivated person *lives* his religion. This distinction is rather important when one comes to examine the effects of religion on the actions of individuals. It is the person who possesses extrinsic religious commitment who appears to be prejudiced, conforming, and authoritarian on many social science studies of religion. The intrinsically motivated person does not exhibit these characteristics.

Allport relates the religious sentiment to the development of the mature personality. He sees no one type but a variety of religious sentiments. The uniqueness of the person finds expression in the uniqueness of each person's religious orientation. The nature of a person's religious orientation at a particular time reflects that person's free response to the situation in which he is. Thus religion can take many forms and can fulfill various functions in a person's life. Just as no one factor determines the human personality, so no one particular factor determines the individual's religious orientation, neither heredity, environment, nor needs.

With this general orientation, we are now prepared to look at the place of religion in the human personality as influenced by factors and attributes of the personality Allport has discussed. Certain aspects of the *organic desires* that a person manifests influence his religion. Religious consciousness can become more intense when a person faces a critical moment, or when he is deprived of something that he desires and needs for his physical well-being. His fears can influence his religious orientation. A person who has a keen and perduring fear of death will have a different religious orientation than a person who rarely thinks about death. A person's concept and relationship to God will strongly color his types of desires and fears. Religion is a deeply human sentiment, and it will manifest itself differently in individuals according to their basic constitutions and organic structures.

The religious expression of the person will also be influenced by the factor of *temperament,* which Allport points to in his construction of the personality. William James in his *Varieties of Religious Experience*[3] developed this influence of temperament by distinguishing between the healthy-minded and the sick-minded personality. The former is the sanguine person who possesses the optimistic view of life. He sees the rosy side of everything. His religion then manifests these same tendencies. He is more apt to speak of God's love, of his Providence, and of a religion of light and comfort. The sick-minded personality takes a pessimistic view. His religion focuses upon sickness, suffering, mortification, self-denial, and death. Religious expressions of these two different temperamental types will vary. They will be satisfied with different conceptions of God. They will be attracted to different forms of ritual expressions. Teachers of religion must be sensitive to these differences. They should also realize their own temperamental dispositions and realize how these have affected their own religious lives. In their teaching they must make provisions for temperamental dispositions that differ from their own.

The religious personality will be greatly influenced by a third factor in personality development Allport singles out. It is the *psychogenic and spiritual values* that a person pursues. Religion is rightly situated in the area of higher concerns, values, and desires. The realm of religion is closely associated with the pursuit of truth, goodness and beauty. Gabriel Moran in his book *Design for Religion* develops a plan for religious education which puts great

108

emphasis on the conscious cultivation of these dimensions of life.[4] He indicates that education through stories, literature, art, and philosophy is actually a form of religious education, and opens the way to a more explicit form. Allport's view of religion is also similar to Paul Tillich's conception of religion as the deeper dimension of each aspect of human life. Religion is concerned with that which is ultimate and deepest in man's human existence.

A *unifying philosophy of life* is another factor in Allport's general theory of personality having a strong bearing on the development of the personality. Allport correctly indicates that a person's philosophy of life need not be religious. But in the case of many individuals this philosophy has a definite religious orientation. Religion often functions as the element which ties all the pieces together and which gives direction to a person's strivings and activities. It provides meaning when a person looks at his life in its entire pattern. Allport's description of this function of personality appears to be a bit too rational. He tends to emphasize only the rational or intellectual aspect of the search for meaning. William James may be more correct in his emphasis upon sentiment, emotion, and feelings in describing religious strivings for ultimate meaning in life.

In the religious education of adults, this need for a unifying philosophy of life cannot be underestimated. The person who comes through the turbulent period of adolescence and youth without some overall philosophy or rationale faces many difficulties in adult life. The religion presented to adults must not be a particular or narrow form of religion. It must attempt to put the pieces of life together and to deal with problems of ultimate meaning. It should not, however, be a religion that has simple solutions to deep and pervasive problems. But it should be able to present the best thinking of religious men on perennial human problems. People do not expect simple solutions to their problems. But they do expect to meet ministers and teachers who have personally grappled with deep human problems and who are in contact with the best thinking and reflections upon these problems.

Another important element in Allport's personality theory that has a strong bearing on religious sentiment is the *individual's response to his culture.* The origins of a person's religious quest are greatly influenced by the particular culture in which he was reared. The young child is introduced to the rituals and the myths of his particular religion. Allport, however, feels that many social scientists exaggerate the influence of culture upon the individual's religion. He points to the many individuals within a culture who do not reflect the belief systems of the particular culture. He maintains that a person will conform to a culture for his own private reasons and will only conform if he sees that this gives significance to his life.

I believe that Allport has made an important distinction in his treatment of the influence of culture upon a person's religious faith. The culture provides the opportunity, but it is the individual who makes the ultimate determination and decision. The faith of each individual is different from that of every other individual. People will respond differently to the same cultural situation. Allport, in attempting to give due consideration to all factors in the human personality that come to bear upon religious faith, thus avoids giving too much emphasis to any particular factor. In this way his study of subjective religion, or what might be called personal religion, provides an antidote to the treatment of religion by social scientists. In studying the common features of the religion of large groups of people, many social scientists tend to forget and do not allow for the uniqueness of each person's religious expression. The religious educator, who by profession is dealing with personal faith, will find Allport's insights and distinctions particularly enlightening and helpful.

In my treatment of Allport's theory of personality, I explained the three processes that he views as essential to the mature personality. The self to be mature must ever be expanding; it might be able to look at itself objectively; and it must have some sense of unity. It should be clear that religious sentiment can aid a person in these three processes of expansion, objectification and unification. Religion aids the process of *self-expansion.* Religion makes the person less concerned with himself and more interested in the good and welfare of others. The prophetic dimension of religion urges the person to become actively involved in the pursuit of justice and fairness in society. It is true that religion can also be used as an instrument for narrowing a person's interests to the private affair of his own soul. Excessive individualism in religion as elsewhere, however, is to be deplored. The predominant thrust of religion is toward more concern with others and the other.

The religious sentiment can aid a person to look at himself objectively, and thus it can foster the process of *self-objectification* that Allport sees as another essential process in the development of the mature personality. The religious person is given to meditation, reflection, and contemplation. The religious literature is replete with urgings to know oneself; it presents a picture of the total man with his strengths and weaknesses. Religious rituals are designed to produce a healthy introspection. They are often a mirror in which a person can see in proper dimension the direction of his life. Practices such as confession provide an opportunity for a self-examination and criticism that helps an individual see himself as he is. A true religious sentiment is consistent with the ideal that a person takes himself seriously but not too seriously.

I have already explained the third and final process Allport describes in his theory of personality, the process of *self-integration or integration.* It is clear that the religious sentiment functions well as a force to unite the various aspects of the human personality and also serves to give deeper meaning to human activities and to human life itself.

Characteristics of Mature Religious Faith

Allport's most important contribution to religious psychology lies in his description of the mature religious sentiment, or what I call adult faith or religion. Allport

111

gives a number of attributes whereby mature faith may be distinguished from immature faith. Every religious educator could well examine his own faith in the light of these characteristics. These characteristics also supply guidelines for educators who are involved in adult education or pastoral work. The rest of this chapter will be devoted to a discussion of these characteristics, with practical applications for those involved in religious education.

1. Mature Faith is Well-Differentiated. A person possesses a well-differentiated faith if he accepts his faith reflectively and critically. He is able to see both the good and the bad that have resulted from the religious impulse. A well-differentiated faith is one that has grown and developed over a long period of time. The person has moved from the naive faith of childhood to the more critical faith of the adolescent and then to the full mature faith of the adult. A well-differentiated faith is able to encompass all dimensions of the human person: the rational, the emotional, the volitional, and the mystical. The sign of a well-differentiated faith is the abandonment of the egocentric concerns of childhood faith which views the adoption of faith as merely a matter of conformity to institutional or parental views.

Besides being characterized by critical tendencies, a well-differentiated faith is also a faith in which various parts are ordered. A sign of the immature person is a tenacious clinging to the less important elements of religious expression and a disregard for more serious religious elements. The mature person sees the entire pattern of religion in which essentials are clearly distinguished from accidentals. A study of attitudes among Catholics, conducted a number of years ago, showed that many were more concerned about the laws of fast and abstinence than they were about the Commandment to love all, even enemies. This is clearly a sign of immature and undifferentiated faith.

Religious education can foster a well-differentiated religious faith in various ways. Religious education for adolescents must challenge their critical powers. It must

112

aid young people to move from a second-hand to a first-hand faith based on personal understanding and commitment. Adolescence is a critical time in the development of a truly reflective faith.

Religious education for adults must focus on the entire panoply that is the religious experience of man. Religious education must entail serious grappling with human problems in the light of religious faith. The entire person must be involved in religious experience. Allport thinks that the goal of religious education among adults is to bring them through prayer to a mystical experience, in which they will clearly see the unity and wholeness of life and faith. It is rewarding that in recent years the spiritual energies of adults have been channeled into various types of prayer groups in which individuals give expression to their spiritual visions. Perhaps these are the appropriate forms for adult religious education.

2. Mature Faith is Dynamic. Allport considers the dynamic nature of mature faith as the most important characteristic distinguishing mature from immature faith. Faith is dynamic if it controls and directs the motives and the activities of the person. This faith is not the servant of other desires and instincts. Faith is the force that interprets events and provides the power of motivation in the individual.

It is because of the dynamic character of religious faith that religion has the power to transform lives. Psychologists who have studied religious conversion have attested to the strength that religion has given to people in overcoming difficulties and problems. Though mature religion has this dynamic power, it is neither fanatical nor compulsive. The mature person is not moved to extreme lengths by reason of his religion. He is always in control of his religious faith; he is not controlled by it.

The religious educator can aid a person to develop a dynamic religious faith by means of challenging discussions on a balanced view of life and faith. People have to be led into discussing seriously the role that religion plays in their lives. They have to examine the real influences of faith and

113

to reflect upon what in their lives comes from faith and what does not. It is not easy, but it is important, to disentangle these elements.

3. Mature Faith is Consistently Directive. According to Allport, religion must persistently and consistently direct and transform character. Religion is not mature if it directs activities in some areas but not in others, or if it directs actions at some times and not at other times. Admittedly, the connection between religion and morality is rather complex, but one can expect in the mature person a consistency between what he believes and what he does.

Religious educators can aid persons striving toward greater consistency. Ethical standards cannot be consistently maintained without some motivating force that the idealism of religions provides. The difficulty of ethical living lies in the tenuous connection that exists between thought and action. The educator can make a person consider intellectually the necessity for consistent behavior, but he has little resources with which to bring a person to act with a degree of consistency.

The Values Clarification approach developed by Sidney Simon and others[5] is one program that has come to grips with this question of consistency in actions. Though this program was developed primarily for children and adolescents, it can easily be adapted to the adult level. The great value of this approach is its attempt to bridge the gap between thought and action by bringing about consistency in action as deriving from a person's beliefs and values.

4. Mature Faith has a Comprehensive Character. In this chapter I have spoken of this particular aspect of mature faith. Allport often repeats that persons need a comprehensive philosophy of life. They cannot live properly unless they put some order into their inner life and unless they make some sense of their place in the world. They must feel that they are concerned with matters central to all human existence. They want to be concerned with causes that make a difference. They also need to look at the entire picture of life.

A comprehensive philosophy of life, one that might be

inspired by religious faith, will make for tolerance of the differences found in others. Allport is particularly sensitive to the matter of human tolerance, for he has devoted much of his research into the nature, causes, forms, and remedies for human prejudice.[6] When persons have a comprehensive view of life, they realize that they alone do not possess all possible values and virtues. In fact, no one group can possibly possess all that is of value. This awareness should promote a tolerance for other persons and for groups in society.

Human prejudice is one of the most disturbing facets that confronts religious educators. It is highly embarrassing when prejudice manifests itself in religion classes and discussions, for the nature of religion is opposed to prejudicial attitudes. It is my experience that adult prejudices are more difficult to handle than the prejudices of youth. This is no doubt true because views tend to become hardened as time passes. A realistic religious education makes serious demands upon people to face up to their prejudices. Programs which promote contact and acquaintances between different groups can do much to remove the harmful prejudices that beset much of our society's life and structures.

5. Mature Faith is Integral. Not only must religious faith be comprehensive for Allport, it must also have an integral character. Faith, to be mature, must be integrated into all areas of life and into all of human knowledge. No large area of life must be unconnected with religious faith. An integral faith admits that much of human behavior is determined by influences outside the person. An integral faith also accommodates the problem of evil within a person and within other individuals. In this area can be seen the influence of the individuation theory of Carl Jung upon Allport. This theory attempts to explain one aspect of maturity in terms of persons being able to accommodate within themselves both good and evil.

Allport treats the problem of the integration of science within the religious point of view. Religion is not either anti-scientific or pre-scientific; it is co-scientific. His treatment is not extensive, but it is important. The religious educator should be familiar with views of religion sympathetic to the scientific point of view. The religious psychology of William James is an example of treating religion from an empirical or scientific point of view. Recent efforts to develop a process theology takes into account the physical view of the world expanding and in process. The system of Teilhard de Chardin is still another effort to breach the gap between religion and science that can strongly appeal to persons of scientific mentality.

6. Mature Faith is Heuristic. This is the most important characteristic of mature religious faith. Allport defines a heuristic belief as one held tentatively until it can be confirmed or until it helps discover a more valid belief. For many individuals, faith is more like a working hypothesis in that it helps persons find better and fuller answers to problems of life. The mature person realizes that he must believe and act at times without absolute certainty. He realizes that absolute certainty is rarely found in ordinary life. The life of faith has always a great amount of risks. People like Pascal, James and Newman have pointed this out in their writings. Our lives are guided by probabilities more than we realize. Tillich's remark that the believer is often closer to the agnostic than he thinks gives the gist of Allport's discussion of the heuristic nature of religious faith.

The religious educator can greatly assist persons who are struggling with the problems of adult faith. Doubts often make up a large part of these difficulties. It is important for the religious educator to be aware of the various ways in which individuals validate or justify their faith. Some people validate their faith through rational argumentation of the sort proposed by Anselm or Aquinas. Others validate their faith through immediate experience convincing to them, but not completely understood by others. Still others validate their faith through the pragmatic approach described by William James. Religious faith

116

appears to them to be a more productive option in life. Through it, they acquire strength and find meaning and purpose. Religious educators can fruitfully engage adults in discussions on the validation and justification of faith. It is good for persons to hear and to experience the types of justification that various people give for the life of faith.

Conclusion

As the churches become more involved in the explicit education of adults, I believe that they will turn to the seminal work of Gordon Allport for an understanding of the nature of adult religious faith. Allport is obviously eclectic in his approach to psychology, drawing from the various schools of thought, and keeping various psychological schools in contact with each other. This factor alone should recommend him to educators who want unity in their psychological understanding but who cannot be versed in all the various psychological schools. Allport's *The Individual and His Religion* will remain a classic study as long as men are seriously interested in how religion affects the whole person in his myriad of activities.

References

1. Gordon Allport. *The Individual and His Religion:* A Psychological Interpretation. New York: Macmillan, 1950. My interpretation of Allport's theories leans heavily on this work.
2. Abraham Maslow. *Motivation and Personality.* New York: Harper, 1954.
3. William James. *Varieties of Religious Experience.* London: 1902.
4. Gabriel Moran. *Design for Religion.* New York: Herder and Herder, 1970.
5. Louis Raths. Merrill Harmin, and Sidney Simon, *Values and Teaching,* Columbus, Ohio, Charles Merrill, 1966; Sidney Simon, Leland Howe, and Howard Kirschenbaum, *Values Clarification: A Hand-*

book of Practical Strategies for Teachers and Students.
New York: Hart, 1972.

6. Gordon Allport. *The Nature of Prejudice.* Reading,
Mass.: Addison-Wesley, 1954.

CHAPTER VIII

JAMES FOWLER: PSYCHOLOGIST OF PSYCHOLOGIST OF FAITH DEVELOPMENT

In recent years a most fruitful approach to the study of faith development has been the theory and research of James Fowler. Fowler is associate professor of Theology and Human Development at the Candler School of Theology, Emory University, Atlanta, Georgia. His research was first done at Harvard Divinity School and at Boston College. In a number of articles and interviews Fowler has emphasized that his research is only in its initial stages and needs extensive testing, analysis, and interpretation. Despite the beginning stage of research, the theory has attracted the attention and imagination of religious educators.

Fowler's theory developed through his work with theological students. In order to help his students understand their faith development, he worked out a speculative theory using the ideas of Erikson's psychosocial stages. He was also influenced by the work of Paul Ricoeor's description of development of faith: precritical, critical and postcritical. Robert Bellah's work of religious evolution was his model of how structural theory works, not at the individual level, but at the level of society and culture. Other influences in shaping his thinking includes the works of Paul Tillich and Richard Niebuhr on faith, and the stages theories of Piaget and Kohlberg.

Understanding the speculative origin of this theory also helps to understand some of the questions and criticisms that have been raised about Fowler's work. That the theory did not arise in an inductive manner disturbs researchers in psychology or social sciences. The origin of the theory in working with theological students indicates that the theory will have to be tested with many other groups before the findings can be generalized for the general population. The origins of a theory are important, but more important are its validity, reliability, and generalizability. If Fowler can substantiate these in his empirical research, then he certainly will have made a substantial contribution to our knowledge of faith and its developmental stages.

The Concept of Faith

To understand Fowler's theory of faith development, it is necessary to understand his idea of faith. In his work he uses faith in a broad sense. Faith in his theory is not used in an institutional but rather in a highly personal sense. He calls faith a way of knowing, construing, or interpreting experience. Faith is a human phenomenon, expressing the universal tendency to make meaning and to give coherence to life. Faith is also relational in bringing the person in contact with others, with a community and with transcendent powers or forces. Fowler's definition of faith does not exclude nontheistic faiths in world religions, such as Buddhism and Confucianism, nor various secular faiths, such as scientism or secular humanism. In all of these systems is found the personal construing of the meaning of life.

In speaking of faith Fowler separates the *Outer Structure* of Faith: *World Maintenance*, from the Inner Structure of Faith; Faith As Knowing. *Faith as World Maintenance* is faith in its social and cultural manifestations. A community, a society and a culture is sustained when vision of reality, both earthly and transcendent is shared. Fowler does not develop this aspect of faith extensively, for he is more interested in the psychological dimensions of faith. A number of eminent social scientists have thoroughly examined this dimension of faith. Durkheim views religious faith as a force of social cohesion. Weber interprets religious faith as a meaning system by which cultures preserve and regenerate themselves.

The *Inner Structure of Faith* treats faith as both knowing and construing. Faith as an activity and as a state of existence flows from knowing and is dependent on faith as knowing. This inner structure of faith is seen as a relationship of trust and loyalty to what are considered centers of value and power. Fowler's interest, as well as Kohlberg's, is more centered on the ways and processes of faith than on the content of faith. He is interested in determining the common structural stages of faith that develop during life.

As a religious educator I find Fowler's description of faith unsatisfactory. I admire his attempt to treat both religious and secular faith under one concept. To him faith is a philosophy of life. Both religious faith and secular faith have the same elements. He does not, however, consider what is most distinctive in religious faith. To analyze religious faith, one must examine the human responses of awe, fear, dread, joy, atonement, celebration, redemption, ecstasy, all of which are distinctive to the religious faith experience. Fowler is certainly aware of these dimensions of religious faith. Because of his dependence upon theological and sociological analyses of faith, and because he says nothing of such psychological descriptions of faith as found in James, Jung, Otto, and others, his description of faith becomes less valuable for the religious educator. Fowler has decided on his universalistic conception of faith. This is a distinctive feature of his research and gives it great value. But the religious educator must also be concerned with a concept of faith that is less reductionistic and less intellectualistic.

Research Methodology

Fowler utilizes the semi-clinical interview method pioneered by Piaget and Elkind. Adults are interviewed from one to three hours. The goals of the interviews are:
1. to elicit the content of the respondent's thinking, valuing and feeling about a set of issues with which faith must deal;
2. to get and to clarify the respondent's sense of the path of his or her development of outlook.[1]

With children the interviews are shorter and include doll-play, story completion, and the question-and-answer approach. Religious themes are not introduced into the sessions at the beginning of the interview. Interviews are generally open ended.

The issues discussed in the interviews are not specifically religious. Existential issues which a person must grapple within his or her faith or philosophy of life form the bases for the interviews. Some of these issues include death and afterlife, evil and suffering, meaning of life, the future, grounding of the ethical and moral imperative, beliefs of what is sinful or a violation; beliefs and ideas of religion and specifically religious symbols.[2]

Thus far Fowler has worked with two major samples of the population in deriving or validating his theory. He and his associates interviewed 118 persons over a two-year period from 1972–74. In 1975 he interviewed an additional 109 persons. Though he has not presented the findings on this later sampling, he states that the presence and validity of the stages have been confirmed by this research.. Samples include both male and female, Protestant, Catholics, Jews, and others?

Alfred McBride is rather critical of Fowler's research methodology.[3] He contends that the reported research does not justify the elaborate theory that has been constructed. He calls for much more research, careful delineation of the various stages and a more cautious presentation of findings. It is difficult to comment on Fowler's methodology, mainly because he has told us so little about it. A fuller treatment of this issue will no doubt be forthcoming. Until it is, questions can be raised about the training and skills of the interviewers, the adequacy of the sampling process, the validity and reliability of the instruments used, and the accuracy or the interpretations given to the data collected. Until Fowler presents a clearer exposition of his methodology, it will be impossible for other researchers to corroborate or dispute his findings and his methodology.

Nature of a Faith Stage

Each of the faith stages is a structural whole, a flexible organization of interrelated patterns of operation. Structure for Fowler refers to:

> the pattern of operations or modes of thinking and valuing which are constitutive of the person's ability to use and give form to beliefs, values, ideas and propositions. Structures in this . . . sense could not be translated into systematic theology, but rather into a kind of epistemology of faith.[4]

This view of structure is taken from the work of Piaget and Kohlberg who describe the workings of the mind in terms of the development of structures or powers by which certain mental operations can be performed.

Fowler has developed a number of characteristics or variables for each stage of faith. Each stage has a *locus of authority* or reference by which the person validates or accepts his faith. Each stage has *criteria and modes of appropriation* by which persons arrive at the truth of their faith. The various stages are characterized by different forms of *symbolic and conceptual functioning*. Another characteristic of a stage is the differing ability of persons to take on the *role of others and to achieve identity*. Finally, each stage has its own *challenges* with which faith must contend.[5]

It is through these variables and characteristics that Fowler relates his work to other researchers, such as Piaget, H. S. Sullivan, Kohlberg, Erikson, and Robert Selman. (Selman has done research on role taking.) It is not clear whether these variables come from empirical research or from speculative analysis of the relationship of faith stages to other stage theorists. Fowler's effort to relate his research with others is helpful in giving the unity of the person of faith. However, these various characteristics of the stages bring a complexity to Fowler's treatment of faith which obscures perception of the developing concept of faith. Fowler is so insistent in making connections between his theory and other theories that the distinctiveness of his contribution is often lost sight of.

Fowler claims that what he has established through research is stages in the Piagetian and Kohlbergian sense. The stages are integrated structural wholes, which are hierarchically related. The order of stages is sequential and invariant. Fowler does not claim universality for these stages because of insufficient research. He also does not attach ages to the stages. The ages he gives are average minimal ages—ages below which he has not found a given stage.

In reporting his research Fowler cautions on the use and usefulness of the stages. He looks upon these stages as heuristic instruments for determining how people feel, think, value, and commit themselves in the area of faith. He does not look upon the stages as a value scale to determine the relative worth of any individuals or groups. These cautions are well taken, especially since research has only begun. Also, since Fowler examines the area of cognitive or intellectual faith only, what he says cannot be generalized in the experience of faith and religion.

Description of Faith Stages

Primal Faith Ages 0–3

The faith of the infant and young child is not differentiated from any other dimension of life. Primal faith includes basic trust, courage, and hope, with mixtures of their opposites. In describing this stage Fowler combines the descriptions of basic trust of Erikson and the sensorimotor stage of Piaget. This stage is both preconceptual and prelinguistic.

Intuitive Faith (Intuitive-Projective Faith) Ages 4–7

Intuitive faith has its *locus of authority* in the faith of parents, family and other significant persons. In a secondary sense the language, symbols, and rituals become another locus of authority. Faith is understood not so much through understanding and concepts as through *imitation* of faith expressions. If the deity is *symbolized* in the life of faith, the representations are frequently pre-anthropomorphic. Though children at this age are unable to take the *role* of others, they are gaining a sense of sexual, racial, and perhaps ethnic *identity*. The *challenge* primal faith encounters is anxiety rooted in death. Children begin to realize that their parents will die and that they will need a ground for faith and hope beyond these persons. Where religious faith is present, some deference begins to be paid to powers that transcend parents and significant others.

Fowler's indebtedness to the research of Piaget, Kohlberg, and Erikson is clear in his description of this stage of faith. In this as in other stages Fowler includes the insights of Selman into the advancing stages of role taking in the developing person.[6] The challenge of death a child faces is brilliantly described by Becker in his *Denial of Death*.[7] Becker shows how the awareness of death, entailing finiteness and mortality, is a fundamental concern, at least at an unconscious level, at every stage in life, even in infancy.

Narratizing Faith (Mythic-Literal Faith) Ages 7–11

Narratizing faith includes in its *locus of authority* parents, as well as teachers, religious leaders, customs, traditions, media, books, and ideas of peers. Children use a number of *criteria* to evaluate the sources of faith: similarity of parents' views and of those whom they respect; consistency in affection for them; competency and interesting qualities; and orthodoxy. When *symbols* of the deity are used, they tend to be anthropomorphic emphasizing the power of God to create. Their narrative ability is developed, but they explain myths and symbols literally. Children at this stage can take on the roles and

126

perspectives of others. They gain *identity* through membership in the groups. The *challenge* to narratizing faith are death, illness, and accidents, and other arbitrary elements and forces that impinge on life. Faith through symbols, myths, rituals, music, and heroic figures can sustain children in these challenges by providing identification and affiliation with persons and groups.

Fowler's dependency on Piaget and Selman are clear in his description of this stage of faith. However, though he connects this stage with Erikson's stages of autonomy vs. shame and doubt and initiative versus guilt, he does not bring into his description of faith the challenges that these stages bring to a developing faith perspective. Perhaps these challenges did not show up in the research. But the sample of children in the research is small (only eight in the 1972–74 study). According to Erikson the challenges to faith could cause children to view God as a demanding law giver who threatens the autonomy and will of the person. Faith is also challenged in the moral area when their conscience is developed and when they are aware of wrong and sinful possibilities in their moral life.

Synthetic Faith (Synthetic-Conventional Faith) Age 12–adulthood

The *locus of authority* for synthetic faith is still outside of a person, though each one is personally responsible for accepting faith. Sanctioned authorities are relied upon, as well as custom and consensus of individuals and groups. *Criteria for determining the truth* of faith are feelings and thoughts in accordance with conventionally agreed upon values and beliefs. Thus there continues the reliance on a community which nurtures beliefs and values. In *symbolic and conceptual functioning* synthetic faith is marked by a world view somewhat systematic and validated by external authorities. Faith is expressed in symbols and ideas of many dimensions. Persons can engage in *mutual role-taking* enabling them to collaborate more fully with others. *Identity* comes from belonging to family and ethnic groups and from possessing competences and abilities. The *problems* faith faces at this stage are to provide a helpful synthesis between the individual and the various roles he begins to play. Faith can give coherence and unity to experiences of various roles. Synthetic faith provides a group identity that can aid in forming personal identity.

The intellectualistic bent of Fowler's theory is clearly evident in his description of this stage. Synthetic faith is described as a highly intellectual task. This form of faith develops in adolescence and young adulthood. The relationship between faith and the emotions and conflicts experienced by adolescents and young adults in their faith is missed in his description. Gruber in his study of the religious evolution of adolescent boys and girls has found other crises: increased affectivity, the awareness of evil in the world, conflicts between religious faith and sexual desires, conflict between faith and personal power and serious doubts about faith.[8] Fowler's research appears to be valid if one adopts the Piaget perspective on faith and knowing. But this view of faith does not do justice to insights about the developing person that have been shown in the psychoanalytic tradition of Freud, Jung, Erikson and other psychologists.

An interesting parallel can be drawn between Fowler's latter stages and Niebuhr's description of the relationships between religion and culture.[9] Niebuhr finds three centrist approaches in the history of Christianity relating to Christ and culture. The *synthesist position* develops a coherent synthesis between the demands of religion and culture. The *paradoxical position* accepts and lives with the tensions between the demands of religion and culture. The *transformist or universalist position* views religion to be a force for overcoming tensions by transforming what is in the culture through the power of religion. While Niebuhr sees these to be three separate responses to a problem in social ethics, Fowler finds them to be developing stages in

128

the individual's faith experience. It will take more extensive research to validate the findings that Fowler reports on these three stages.

Individuative Faith (Individuating-Reflexive Faith) 18–adulthood

Typical *loci of authority* for individuative faith are charismatic leaders, ideology, and attention to personal experience and to experience of peers. Personal judgment plays a strong role in determining beliefs. Thus authority becomes internalized. *Criteria* for determining truth are also personal and internal: existential congruence with the developing person. In the area of *symbolic and conceptual functioning* persons begin to be more critically reflective of their faith. Faith is seen as a relative system, often different from others. Symbols are distinguished from what they symbolize. *Mutual role-taking* with other groups is possible. Personal *identity* is no longer derivative. Individuals are aware of their own identities. The existential *challenge* faced in this stage is individualization. To become individuated for Fowler is:

> to find or create identifications and affiliations with ideologically defined groups whose outlook is expressive of the self one is becoming and has become, and of the truth or truths which have come to provide one's fundamental orientation.[10]

According to Fowler persons arrive at this stage of faith when they become aware of the boundaries of their outlook. Individuative faith accepts affiliation with a group and its ideology, while recognizing the reality of relativism.

Fowler gets down to the meaning of faith in his discussion of the challenges dealing with faith. In the other variables or characteristics of faith he appears to confirm the research of others. For this reason my critical remarks on his theory are most often directed to this discussion. I find it difficult to accept that the transition from synthetic faith to individuative faith is exclusively or chiefly the intellectual task Fowler describes. The research of Erikson, Kenniston and Yankelovich on young adults presents a wide range of emotional and cultural challenges with which the young adult must deal in forging a personal faith. Fowler's prototypical challenge for this stage appear appropriate for seminarians, divinity students, and budding theologians. From the research I have mentioned it is clear that young adults have serious faith problems in such areas as authority, sexuality, the evils of institutionalized religion, the urgency of other developmental tasks, the desire for simple solutions to complex problems. Most young adults are not seriously challenged by differing life-styles and faith-styles but are challenged by the style of life and faith in their faith communities. In the description of this faith stage, as in the others, Fowler's research seems to confirm the theories of such cognitive structuralist as Kohlberg, Piaget and Selman; but he does not find evidence for the findings of psychoanalytically oriented researchers. I find it hard to believe that he did not raise any of these concerns in his interviewing.

Conjunctive Faith (Paradoxical-Consolidative Faith) Age 30 minimum

The *locus of authority* is fully internalized. Tradition, scriptures, customs, ideologies are accepted as normative but do not determine the person's faith. The *criteria* for arriving at the truth and adequacy of faith lie in the combination of judgment and the cumulated experiences of other people. Conjunctive faith accepts the tensions between conflicting loyalties, for it accepts paradox as an essential characteristic of all truth. In *conceptual functioning* conjunctive faith is committed to the absoluteness of truth but accepts the fact that our knowledge of truth is partial, limited, and often opposed to the views of others.

130

Symbols are understood critically as symbols originating in a specific place and time and as relative representations of absolute truth. At this stage of development persons can take the *roles* of other persons and groups in their full complexity. Conjunctive faith can *identify* with groups, even though it realizes their weaknesses and strengths; it also has a social awareness beyond class norms and interests. Existential *challenges* for persons arise from an awareness of the limits of personal and communal identifications. Faith must confront the sense of loneliness resulting from the realization of the gaps of separation from those closest and from groups that one is involved with. Faith also faces the challenge of being ethically responsible even in the face of egocentricity, ignorance, and finiteness. Faith, according to Fowler, is a volitional act of paradoxical commitment that takes its own doubt and despair seriously.

Fowler's description of conjunctive faith is impressive. The influence of existentially oriented theologians such as Tillich and Niebuhr is clear. In the light of recent research on adult development, however, one can question the sufficiency and adequacy of Fowler's description of the challenges to faith. An increasing sense of finiteness and loneliness is found in this research. But other crises are also reported: physical aging, career dissatisfaction, the inevitability of death, danger of stagnation, questioning of life structure, style and commitments, and a renewed search for the meaning of life. The description of conjunctive faith would be enhanced by relating it to the other crises described by more psychologically and psychoanalytically oriented researchers. One gets the impression (and it can only be an impression until it can be checked by looking at more of Fowler's data) that the theological stance and the cognitive structuralist viewpoint that Fowler has adopted either dictate what he finds relevant in the data or are used as filters for interpreting the data. It would be interesting if other researchers, trained outside

Fowler's presuppositions, would arrive at the same descriptions of the various stages.

Universalizing Faith Age 40 minimum

The *locus of authority* is personal judgment and disciplined intuition into the ultimate conditions of existence. Persons at this stage participate in or are permeated by transcendent being. The *criteria and modes of appropriating truth* result in a synthesis that reconciles differing truths without denying particular and unique contributions of each viewpoint. *Symbolic and conceptual understanding* are of secondary importance, for life is directly and nonmediately lived and understood. Universalizing faith can take the *role* of the transcendent and express loyalty to it. Persons can *identify* with the "Commonwealth of Being" and with the universal community. Fowler describes a number of *challenges* that faith at this stage must face: danger of absorption in the All, relating to persons at other stages, temptations to pride and self-deception, danger of ethical and political paralysis, misunderstandings and slanders, and the burden of being a mediator, teacher or model for others.

In discussing the similarities and differences between his faith stages and the traditions of spirituality, Fowler points out that this is not *the* mystical stage but does include the mystical person. It is clear that Fowler's description of this stage has numerous mystical traits and characteristics. Actual descriptions of case studies of persons of faith in their own words are lacking, making it impossible to understand this and other stages. Fowler should provide us with the same rich personal descriptions that Goldman provided in his developmental study on religious thinking. Examples of these stages will come to life only if they are concretized with descriptions. Because these are lacking, apparent gaps in data collection and interpretation are found in Fowler's presentation of his findings.

Faith Development Theory and Religious Education

Despite the questions and criticisms raised about Fowler's theory of faith development, religious educators can utilize this approach to faith with great profit in the theory and practice of religious education. Before the relevance of the theory for various age groups is studied, a number of general implications are noted.

Fowler has provided a valuable model for understanding the nature of faith and its developmental stages. He has provided goals for religious education. Mature faith must be personal, reflexive, synthetic, tension-bearing, and immediate. His delineation of the stages of faith cautions the educator that faith is a life-long pilgrimage dependent on organic, developmental, and social factors. Fowler also indicates some of the general means that might be used in education for faith: Faith is to be challenged by the examples of the faith of others and by facing various crises of faith.

Implications for Childhood Religious Education

The necessity for faith-filled personal relationships with the infant and young child upon which to build religious faith is the most important implication in this area. Religious faith needs a strong basic faith, hope, and courage in facing life's problems. Death and other crises are to be presented to children as realities. Fowler's research makes imperative the growth of family religious education programs. Earliest development of religious faith is dependent upon the quality of the relationships between the child and parents and significant others.

Education during childhood takes place under the sponsorship of a community of religious faith. Fowler recommends that "in the interaction that leads to development, important roles are played by the ethical teaching, ritual practices, scriptures, laws, music, art and worship of the community."[11] Religious educators such as Gabriel

Moran and John Westerhoff have stressed the importance of these forms of faith socialization. Fowler's research gives empircal validation to the importance of enculturation in faith development.

Implications for Adolescent Religious Education

Adolescent faith must make the transition from narratizing faith to synthetic and individuative faith. The religious community through its educational efforts must sustain the growing person in the midst of the transitional crises leading to a mature faith. Religious education should challenge a young person to move away from a faith dependent upon others to a more personal synthesis reflecting the individual style of the believer.

Though Fowler in his description of faith stages emphasizes growth in cognitive perspective and conceptual functioning, he does provide a concrete and total model of faith development through his description of the pilgrimage in faith of Malcolm X.[12] Malcolm arrives at mature faith through the resolution of highly emotional conflicts, of which one aspect is growth of intelligence.

This example of faith pilgrimage challenges religious educators to present to young people stories of faith that can shed light on their own experiences. It is also helpful for educators to discuss their own faith pilgrimage. Through reading and listening to faith stories, young people will gain perspective as to their own crises and development of faith. The lives of the saints provided this insight and inspiration for past generations and the lives of contempory persons need to be developed to light the paths for faithful persons in their pilgrimage through life.

Implications for Adult Religious Education

Though Fowler's theory has implications for pre-adult religious education, its strongest relevance is for adult religious education as Gilmour has indicated in an appraisal of Fowler's work.[13] Most of the persons in his studied samples were adults. Fowler has also done great

134

service for adult religious educators by revealing the adult stages of faith. This calls for an education in the faith, through formal and informal processes, throughout life.

Adult education for faith development needs people to challenge and to increase dissonance where there is complacency or refusal to grow. The adult education that suits this model is not the banking education Paulo Freire criticizes but education to raise critical consciousness and to inspire action.[14] Religious education for adults must include a personal challenge for growth and a critical look at the myths in contemporary culture.

From Fowler's research it is clear that an adult needs this type of critical faith. But positive aspects of the earlier stages of faith need to be present in adult faith and provided for in adult religious education. Faith must have the element of trust; it must be connected to a religious community; it must provide a synthesis of meanings for life; it must be a force for withstanding tensions of life. The challenges of faith of the earlier stages remain for life.

Ecumenical education described by Gabriel Moran gives a final impetus to adult religious education coming from Fowler's research.[15] Fowler has developed a concept of faith that transcends religious traditions and extends into secular faiths. Athough this reductionistic tendency does not do justice to religious faith, it does enable us to be aware of the similarities between secular and religious faith. Working within this broad concept of faith, people will be cognizant of the world-wide and ecumenical aspects of all faith and education.

Conclusion

Though Fowler's work is still sketchy and tentative and difficult to understand, it is a fruitful heuristic tool for religious educators. Examined and applied with the cautions that he and others have appended, it can bring greater understanding of what faith development is and provide realistic goals for a lifelong religious education.

References

1. James W. Fowler, "Stages in Faith: The Structural-Developmental Approach." In T. Hennessy, *Values and Moral Development*. Paulist, 1977, p. 179.
2. Fowler, op. cit., p. 181.
3. Alfred McBride, "Reaction to Fowler: Fear about Procedure. In T. Hennessy, *Values and Moral Development*, pp. 211–218.
4. James W. Fowler, op. cit., p. 178.
5. Fowler, op. cit., pp. 186–188.
6. Robert L. Selman, "A Developmental Approach to Interpersonal and Moral Awareness in Young Children: Some Educational Implications of Levels of Social Perspective-Taking." In T. Hennessy, *Values and Moral Education*, p. 167.
7. Ernest Becker, *The Denial of Death*. Macmillan, 1973.
8. Alois Gruber, "Differences in Religious Evolution of Adolescent Boys and Girls." In *Research in Religious Psychology*. Brussels: Lumen Vitae Press, 1957.
9. H. Richard Niebuhr, *Christ and Culture*. Harper, 1951.
10. Fowler, Op. cit., p. 199.
11. James W. Fowler, "James Fowler Talks with Lisa Kuhmerker about Faith Development." *Moral Education Forum,* vol. 3, no. 3, June 1978, p. 6.
12. James W. Fowler, "Faith, Liberation and Human Development." Thirkield-Jones Lectures, Gammon Theological Seminary, 1974.
13. Stephen C. Gilmour, "What Does Fowler Have to Say to Adult Educators?" *Living Light*, vol. 13, no. 4 (Winter 1976).
14. Paulo Freire, *Pedagogy of the Oppressed*. Herder and Herder, 1970.
15. Gabriel Moran, *Design for Religion: Toward Ecumentical Education*. Herder and Herder, 1970.

CHAPTER IX

PSYCHOLOGISTS OF ADULT DEVELOPMENT

Until recently developmental psychology included only the study of developmental stages in childhood and adolescence. Adulthood was viewed as a period of sameness, stability, and constancy. This widespread view faces a serious challenge today due to an emerging research literature which relates personality, aging, and theories of adult development. Data and theories are now available that describe the various changes, conflicts and developments that take place during the adult years. A review of some of this literature will be helpful, I hope, for those involved in religious ministry to adults. A religious ministry can be successful in dealing with adults only if it recognizes adult needs and is aware of the processes of change that adults experience. Only if these needs and processes are known, can religious ministers and educators develop strategies to help adults find solutions to the problems and dilemmas that they face in the course of their life development.

Early Theories of Adult Development

Before the recent surge of interest in adult development some psychologists developed theories about stages of the life cycle beyond adolescence. The theories of Jung, Buhler and Erikson are based on inferences drawn from clinical or empirical observations. They have not been rigorously tested and supported by empirical research.

Charlotte Buhler based her theory of adult development on a study of biographies and autobiographies.[1] She delineated five phases: 0–15 child at home: prior to self determination of goals; 15–25 preparatory expansion and experimental self determination of goals; 25–45 culmination: definite and specific self determination of goals; 45–65 self-assessment of the results of striving for these goals; 65 and up experience of fulfillment or failure: remaining years spent either in continuance of previous activities or a return to need-satisfying orientations of earlier years. Two great tendencies characterize adult develop-

138

ment in this view: expansion and contraction. At mid-life these two contradictory tendencies collide to present a turning point or crisis in the form of an assessment of goals that one has reached or failed to reach in one's life.

The biographies that Buhler and her associates studied were written in Vienna in the 1930's. Though a contraction of interests appears to be a part of adult development, this occurs much later in American culture today. All theories of adult development must face the problem of cultural determination. As theories move away from a biological base to embrace cultural dimensions, they lose their universality and become culturally conditioned.

Carl Jung in his theorizing about the stages of life went beyond the biologically based stages delineated by Freud. To the anal, oral, genital, latency, and puberty stages of life he added the stage of youth (puberty to middle years), a period of intolerance and fanaticism around the age of 50, and a period of inner spiritual and religious development after 50 and until death.[2] The second half of life affords the opportunity to deepen spiritual and religious values by reflecting on the meaning of life and death. Jung notes that the only schools for 40 year olds have been the great religions where people are prepared for old age, death, and eternity.

This tendency towards inwardness in the second half of life has been noted also by present day psychologists. A religious ministry to adults, middle-aged and aged should develop opportunities and strategies to enable people to deepen their spiritual resources through prayer, group sharing, group discussion, and worship. Only through developing these resources can adults resolve the crises of disappointment, isolation, stagnation, and despair that often come in the middle and late years.

The Neo-Freudian psychoanalyst, *Erik Erikson*, has presented a well known approach to the human developmental process.[3] The human life cycle consists of a series of eight critical turning points reaching from birth to death. The five earlier turning points correspond to the five stages of Freud. Erikson's description of these stages emphasizes the influence of psychosocial factors rather than the psychosexual factors that Freud stressed. To these stages Erikson has added the three developmental crises of adulthood: intimacy versus isolation in early adulthood; generativity versus stagnation in middle adulthood; and integrity versus despair and disgust in late adulthood.

The intimacy crisis in early adulthood is successfully resolved through close intimate relationships with spouse and friends and the expression of warm and deep feelings for them. It is unsuccessfully resolved through isolation from friends, spouse, and children, the avoidance of contact on an intimate basis, and formalized relationships with others. The generativity crisis in middle adulthood is successfully resolved through a sense of continuity with future generations and the investment of energy and ideas into new projects and interests. It is unsuccessfully resolved by preoccupation with self and an impoverishment of interests. The integrity crisis in late adulthood is successfully resolved through the acceptance of responsibility for one's life and the affirmation of the meaningfulness of one's life, in the face of sickness and impending death. It is unsuccessfully resolved through feelings of depression, an emphasis on the past, and an extreme fear of death.

Though Erikson's description of the life cycle has received general acceptance, theorists have attempted to define the crucial issues of middle age and adulthood more precisely. *Robert Peck* presents seven crucial issues in these two periods.[4] The crises in middle age are: valuing wisdom versus valuing physical powers; socializing versus sexualizing in human relationships; emotional flexibility versus emotional impoverishment (as parents die, children leave home, and friendships are ended, can the person develop other relationships?); mental flexibility versus mental rigidity. The crises in old age according to Peck are: ego differentiation versus work-role preoccupation (can interests be developed in retirement?): body transcendence versus body preoccupation (can the person transcend the frailty of his/her own aging body?); ego transcendence versus ego preoccupation (can persons transcend the significance of their lives beyond their lifetimes?).

The implications of Erikson's (and Peck's) approach to the human life cycle is rich in its implications for a religious ministry to adults. Religious education, worship, and fellowship can provide the context and means in which the various dimensions of human relationships can be studied, explored, experienced, and celebrated. The adult religious person gains through religious life the motivation and opportunity to care for family, friends, and all persons. Religion places the emphasis upon the quest for wisdom, the spiritual and interpersonal dimension of sexuality, and the call of all men to love and care for others. Religion provides older adults with an integrating vision of life in which a person is of more value than his work, in which there is a genuine hope for the transcendence of body and self into an eternal life with God.

Recent Research in Adult Development

In recent years a number of research studies have been reported that attempt to describe the human life span. None of these studies try to describe the entire life span. In some ways these studies confirm and extend the earlier research. In other ways this research adds precision, clarifications, distinctions, and qualifications to the research of Erikson and others. Not all of this research can be reviewed in this short chapter. But I shall try to review the research which appears to be the most promising and which has particular relevance for religious ministry.

Bernice Neugarten and associates in a large field study in Kansas City studies a sample of 710 people in the mid-1950's.[5] They concentrated on middle life and the sample was from 40 to 90 years old. The results of the study indicate the complex task it is to develop an integrated body of theory that encompasses the entire life span. The study included men and women from various social classes, thus providing important variables for investigation.

The salient issues of adulthood at a level of generality were found to be these: individuals' use of experience; their structuring of the social world in which they live; their perspectives of time; the ways in which they deal with work, love, time, death; changes in self-concept and changes in identity as they face the successive contingencies of marriage, parenthood, career advancement and decline, retirement, widowhood, illness, and personal death. These issues take different forms at different periods in adulthood.

Neugarten found that the middle years of life—probably the fifties for most people—represent an important turning point because of a restructuring of time and the development of new perspectivies on self, time, and death. Mental life at this time becomes more reflective and contemplative and self evaluation and review become characteristic forms of mental life. Differences in age groups were found: 40 year olds found the environment as inviting boldness and risk taking; 60 year olds viewed it as complex and dangerous. Important differences among the sexes were found: men became more receptive to affiliative and nurturant promptness; women became more responsive toward and less guilty about aggressive and egocentric impulses.

In these studies Neugarten developed her concept of the social clock, the prescriptive timetable for the ordering of life events. Most people carry within themselves a pattern for the proper time for events to occur: a time when men and women are expected to marry, a time to raise children, a time to retire. People consider themselves early, late or on time with regard to family and occupational events. This timeclock is superimposed upon the biological clock.

Thus the major marking times in adult life are social rather than biological.

While Neugarten studied the age group between 40 and 90 and concluded that no clear pattern for the life cycle could be differentiated, *Roger Gould* has delineated clear phases in the adult years.[6] His sample consisted of 525 men and women between the ages of 16 and 60. It should be noted that Gail Sheehy, in her book *Passages* utilized this research extensively in her description of the predictable crises of adulthood.[7]

Gould has differentiated six stages in adult development. The youngest group (16–18) was concerned with escape from parental dominance and expressed feelings of anxiety and dependence as they prepared to leave the parental home. The next group (18–22) began to substitute friends for family as they continued to grow independent of the family. They also began to relate more intimately with their peers. The group from ages 22–28 felt established and autonomous with regard to their families. They were engaged in mastering their careers. Most of their emotional life was centered upon their spouses.

The first real crisis in adulthood was manifested in the group between the ages of 29 and 34. They were often questioning what they were doing and why they were doing it. In their careers they realized that their wills alone were not sufficient to accomplish all their dreams and aspirations. They desired to be accepted by their spouses for what they were. In the group from ages 35 to 43 there was the continued look within but this time with a less urgent tone. Time began to press upon this group as they realized that they had little time to influence their adolescent children. In their work they had a sense of last chance to make it. In the years from 44 to 50 people came to grips with time and with their stable personalities. They became more actively involved in the lives of their children. They were eager to have social contacts and friends. They looked for support and sympathy from their spouses. By the 50's there was a mellowing and warming age. People began to look to their children for approval and became more concerned with problems of health.

The sample used by Gould consisted of white middle class persons. In fact most studies on adult development have used similar samples. Thus care must be used in generalizing these findings to other populations. The emphasis in Gould's study is upon changing self concept, attitudes towards parents, peers, spouse, friends, work attitudes and perceptions of time in one's life. Other variables were not considered: death, retirement, religion, leisure, sexuality, and community. The existence of so many variables in adult development points to the extreme difficulty in developing a single theory that would encompass all adults.

One important finding in Gould's research is the existence of a mid-life crisis in adulthood. This finding is confirmed by many other studies.[8] Jacques has argued that this crisis is brought on by the awareness of one's own impending death. It would appear that a religious ministry to adults should address itself in a serious manner to this developmental crisis. Unfortunately, as with many other problems, people do not seek help until it is too late. In religious life there is bountiful support available for people in a mid-life crisis. Prayer groups, adult education programs concerning this problem, marriage encounters, individual counseling are forms of ministry that can aid people at this time in llfe. All the research indicates that the root of the problem is an inner or spiritual crisis. Perhaps it is time for religions to become the schools for forty year olds that Jung proposed.

Another theory of psychosocial development in adults has been presented by *Daniel Levinson* and associates.[9] There are a number of similarities with Gould's theory but there are also a number of differences. Levinson studied forty men all of whom were aged 35–45. Men came from four occupational groups: blue and white collar workers in industry; business executives; academic biologists; and novelists. Levinson has contructed a theory of adult male development over the age span of about 20–45.

In brief Levinson's stages are the following: *Leaving the Family* (Starting at age 16–18 and ending at 20–24); *Getting in the Adult World* (early 20's to 27–29); *Age Thirty Transition* (28–32); *Settling Down* (from early 30's to age 39–41); *Mid-Life Transition* (late 30's to early 40's); *Restabilization* (around age 45).

Levinson has added some important refinements to the theories of Gould and others. He has found various patterns of *Getting into the Adult World*. Some persons remain in the occupation which they chose in their 20's. Others around 30 decide to enter a new career because the first was too constraining or a violation or betrayal of an earlier dream. Still others live a rather transient, unsettled life in the 20's and do not build a firm life structure until their 30's.

Becoming one's own man and making it in the adult world demands, according to Levinson, a mentor. This is the older person who takes the younger man under his wing, invites him into a new occupational world, shows him around, imparts his wisdom, cares for, sponsors and criticizes the younger man. The younger man reciprocates with appreciation, respect, gratitude, love and identification. By the time the young man has reached 40 he has abandoned the mentor relationship. It should be noted that Hennig and Jardim have found evidence of a mentor-mentee relationship in women who have become successful top executives in corporations.[10]

Finally, Levinson indicates some of the major issues within the mid-life crisis. There is a sense of bodily decline and the more vivid recognition of one's mortality. This sense can bring greater freedom in experiencing and thinking about one's own death and also greater compassion in responding to others. There is also a sense of aging, which means to be old rather than young. A third issue is the polarity of masculine and feminine. The integration and emergence of the more feminine aspects of the self are more possible at mid-life.

The final theory of adult development to be discussed in this review is that of the psychiatrist *George Vaillant.*[11] The sample used in this study is a narrower one than that used by Levinson and others. It is basically a follow-up study of men who were healthy and promising undergraduates at an elite college between the years 1939 and 1942. Vaillant develops at length the various mechanisms these men used in coping with problems which they faced in life. He sums up his findings in a chapter entitled *"The Adult Life Cycle—In One Culture."*

Vaillant basically adheres to the life cycle theory of Erikson with one major addition, the addition of a stage called Career Consolidation. Vaillant found dramatic identity crises in adolescence to be extremely rare and not associated with psychological health. He found that to fail at intimacy was to forfeit mastery in the next stages of the adult life cycle. Marrying too young, before a capacity for intimacy was developed, boded poorly for a successful marriage. Vaillant places the stage of Career Consolidation in the thirties and finds this stage connected with the acquisition, assimilation and finally casting off of mentors.

Vaillant places the generativity crisis at the heart of the mid-life crisis, and terms it a second adolescence. He believes however that the crisis dimension has been exaggerated by such studies as Gail Sheehy's *Passages*. He observes that the high drama found in the lives of people in Sheehy's book was rarely found in the men he studied. The final crisis that Erikson terms integrity versus despair or disgust Vaillant sees in terms of keeping the meaning and rigidity. The fifties are a quieter time when men see a new generation taking over. Many men at this time developed a capacity to care for others that they did not previously believe possible.

I have found the Vaillent study particularly interesting

because it is the only study that examined the religious development of adults with any degree of seriousness. The modal pattern to religious development found in this study was this: relatively high involvement in adolescence, a decline in the decades between 20 and 40, then a gradual increase. In their view of God these men replaced the God who binds moral conscience with a God who is an invisible trusted power behind the universe. True to his psychoanalytic orientation Vaillant explains the reappearance of religion in the fifties as the rediscovery of internalized parents. He points to the research of Ana-Maria Rizzuto that has elucidated the extraordinary congruence between an adult's felt and experienced image of God and the internalized parents.[12] Even though he is a social scientist, Vaillant accepts as an apt description of adult development the Christian metaphor of Pilgrim's Progress, depending as it does on mysterious growth within, inspired by equally mysterious forces without. This concept has been fully developed by William J. Brouwsma in his article on "Christian Adulthood".[13]

Discussion And Implications of the Findings

Research in adult development is obviously at a rather primitive stage. Most psychologists view the popularization of limited findings such as Sheehy attempted to be both premature and dangerous. With the book's journalistic tendency to stress the dramatic, its emphasis on the resolution of mid-life crisis through divorce and remarriage, its exclusive attention on an upper middle class professional population, and its failure to consider the later stages of human development, it presents an incomplete and selective account of adult development. Sufficient research is not yet available to generalize from limited studies to the entire population, even within a given culture.

The research on adult development has not directed itself sufficiently to the study of women and social classes other than the middle class. In this regard Sheehy's work is somewhat of a break-through, with the amount of attention that it gives to detailing developmental problems of woman. Sheehy shows how conflicts develop between husbands and wives as men turn from careers to family and community interests and women turn from family to career interests. It is difficult to speculate what the results of more attention to the study of women and social classes other than the middle class would be, but certainly these findings would add further clarifications and modifications.

As I have indicated in this chapter, it is my belief that the religious educator and minister can profit from a study of research in adult development. It is the opinion of many people that religious ministry, and especially religious education, has been overly concentrated upon children and adolescents. The exclusive adoption of the schooling model for religious education may be largely responsible for this. Perhaps this lack of attention to adults can be better understood in the light of a dearth of information about what is happening in adult lives and what their real needs are. There is less excuse for this today as psychologists and other social scientists have presented theories and research on adult development and needs. Major works reporting this research have also appeared.[14] The time may be ripe for a conference of researchers, theorists, and practitioners, similar to the Marriotsville Conference to examine all aspects of religious ministry to adults.[15]

References

1. Charlotte Buhler (Ed.), *The Course of Human Life.* NY: Springer, 1968.
2. Carl Jung. "The Stages of Life." In C. Jung, *Modern Man in Search of a Soul.* Harcourt, 1933.
3. Erik Erikson, Childhood and Society. Norton, 1950;

''Reflections on Dr. Borg's Life Cycle.'' In E. Erikson (Ed.), *Adulthood.* Norton, 1978.

4. Robert Peck, ''Psychological Developments in the Second Half of Life.'' In J. Anderson (Ed.), *Psychological Aspects of Aging.* Washington: American Psychological Association, 1955.

5. Bernice Neugarten, *Personality in Middle and Late Life.* NY: Atherton, 1964; *Middle Age and Aging.* University of Chicago Press, 1968.

6. Roger Gould, ''The Phases of Adult Life: A Study in Developmental Psychology.'' *American Journal of Psychiatry,* 1972, vol. 129, pp. 521–531.

7. Gail Sheehy, *Passages: Predictable Crises of Adult Life.* Dutton, 1976.

8. Elliot Jacques, ''Death and the Mid-Life Crisis.'' *International Journal of Psychoanalysis,* 1965, Vol. 46, pp. 502–514; Orville Brim, ''Theories of the Male Mid-Life Crisis.'' *Counseling Psychologist,* 1976, vol. 6, pp. 2–9; Daniel Levinson, Periods in the Adult Development of men: Ages 18–45.'' *Counseling Psychologist,* 1976, vol. 6, pp. 21–25.

9. Daniel Levinson, op. cit.

10. Margaret Hennig and Anne Jardim, *The Managerial Woman.* Doubleday, 1976.

11. George Vaillant, *Adaptation to Life.* Little, Brown and Co., 1977.

12. Ana-Maria Rizzutto, ''Object Relations and the Formation of Image of God.'' *British Journal of Medical Psychology,* 1974, vol. 47, pp. 83–89.

13. William J. Brouwsma, ''Christian Adulthood.'' In *Adulthood,* E. Erikson (Ed.). Norton, 1978.

14. Doughlas Kimmel. *Adulthood and Aging.* Wiley, 1974.; Alan Knox *Adult Learning and Development.* Jossey-Bass, 1977.

15. Berard Marthaler and Margaret Sawicki (Eds.), *Catechesis: Realities and Visions: A Symposium on the Catechesis of Children and Youth.* Washington: United States Catholic Conference, 1977.

PSYCHOLOGY AND RELIGIOUS EDUCATION: A BIBLIOGRAPHIC ESSAY

In the previous chapters of this book I have attempted to present briefly the theory and research of a number of psychologists and to draw implications from them for the theory and practice of religious education. In this chapter my intention is to bring this material up-to-date by reviewing some recent and significant developments in the psychological foundations of religious education. Thus this chapter provides resources for current discussions in psychology and religious education. It is hoped that this essay will enhance the use of the book for both theorists and practitioners.

I. The Relationship Between Psychology and Religious Education

Religion.   The nature of the religious has been the subject of much scholarly work in a number of disciplines. A most profound exploration of the individual religious life is found in the works of John Dunne.[1] Dunne's exploration of the religious takes him through philosophy, theology, psychology, and literature. His emphasis is on understanding the dramatic, personal and interpersonal dimensions of the religious journey. This approach to the religious complements the more intellectual approach found in other scholars of religion.

Although Dunne's work has not yet affected the field of religious education as much as it should, his ideas provide an understanding of story and biography which can be important components of religious education. Dunne's work has a psychological analogue in the intensive journal

151

method developed by Ira Progoff.[2] Though this approach does not have an explicit religious dimension, it can be adapted to persons with a religious view of life.

The understanding of religion from a psychological perspective has been enhanced by the thorough treatment of Spilka, Hood, and Gorsuch.[3] This work has both theoretical and empirical strengths. It reviews the various psychological approaches to religion, research on religious development, and such special topics as religious experience, mysticism, conversion, and morality. The authors also treat the role religion plays in mental disorders. Religion is seen to be a haven, a therapy, and a hazard. Also, Gorman offers an excellent reader of basic writers in psychology and religion.[4]

Psychology. The psychological viewpoint that has generated the most interest among religious educators is that of the developmentalists, especially Kohlberg and Fowler. Psychoanalytic thought has also influenced the work of religious educators. A most valuable resource for exploring these recent developments is the collection of papers of the Semanque Conference convened by C. Brusselmans.[5] Both European and North American perspectives were brought to bear on development and psychological issues. The material in this book is most helpful for educators of children, adolescents, and adults because all of the authors offer suggestions from their work for the practice of religious education. Without a doubt this volume is the most important work to appear in psychology and religious education. Reference will be made in this chapter to several significant articles in this collection.

Education and Religious Education. It has been long recognized that there are many theories of education. My work in attempting to examine the philosophical foundations of adult education resulted in six theoretical approaches which are also applicable to general education.[6]

They are: liberal, progressive, behaviorist (socialization theory), humanistic, radical, and analytic. The behaviorist and humanistic approaches have the strongest bases in psychology. Differences among these theories arise from an analysis of objectives or goals, content-method, and teacher-student relationships. In a later work I applied these theories to the field of adult religious education.[7]

Other religious educators have employed psychology in their theories of religious education. Moran, after criticizing developmental theories, described a religious education theory similar to social science research in religious development.[8] A more sympathetic use of developmental psychology for religious educators is offered by Miller who shows an awareness of both the strengths and weaknesses of these theorists.[9] Groome draws on the theories of Piaget and Fowler in developing a highly influential theory of Christian shared praxis.[10] Barker offered a typology of theories of religious education including a psychological type based on the work of Lewis Joseph Sherrill and Joseph Goldbrunner.[11] Finally, in his school based theory of religious education Grimmitt makes extensive use of psychological research.[12]

Moral Education.   The work of psychologists is particularly important for moral education in both secular and religious settings. In a book on moral education,[13] I have devoted a chapter to the implications of psychological theories on moral education. Behaviorists help us understand the power of environment and reinforcement in the learning of moral behavior. Psychoanalysis focuses on the power of internal dynamics and drives to form moral persons. The cognitive developmentalism of Piaget and Kohlberg explains the moral progress through particular stages, as described in an earlier chapter of this book. Social learning theories attend to the power of interactive learning in social environments. Finally, humanistic or personalistic theories help us understand that moral development includes all the above processes and more.

II. Social Learning Theory and Religious Education

What has become clear about behaviorist psychology is that there are at least two forms of behaviorism: the radical behaviorism of B. F. Skinner, which was discussed earlier in this book, and the moderate or modified behaviorism of such social learning theorists as Bandura, Walters, Aronfreed, and Rushton.[14] It is the latter form of behaviorism that has value in understanding processes in religious education.

Moderate behaviorism can be consonant with a religious point of view of the person because it regards the environment as but one element in shaping beliefs, attitudes, and behaviors. This theory recognizes the inner person as an autonomous individual. What this view stresses is that environmental factors are highly influential in personal development as well as in educational settings. James M. Lee has utilized this moderate behaviorism in developing a truly comprehensive theory of religious education.[15]

Psychologically oriented social learning theories appeal to such concepts as parent identification, internalization of values, dependency, frustration, and aggression in order to explain the moral development of persons. This theory does not present an age related sequence of stages. According to the theory, persons grow in affection and develop behaviors through the interaction of internal emotional dynamics with particular environmental factors. Changes in individuals are brought about not so much through internal maturation or development as through sudden changes in social situations, family structures, peer group expectations, or other environmental factors.[16]

The cognitive branch of social learning theory is found

in the works of Bandura and Rushton.[17] The major focus of these theories is upon the power of models to shape human learning and behavior. Bandura has attempted to show that the mere exposure to the behavior of a model without any reward for imitation of it is sufficient for learning the behavior. In this viewpoint learning through modeling is not reducible to conditioning or learning through reinforcement.

In recent years the thinking of religious educators on moral development has been dominated by Kohlberg's cognitive developmentalism. Since this theory has increasingly come under fire by scholars, it is important for religious educators to broaden their thinking on moral development. The various processes described by social learning theorists make educators more aware of internal, interpersonal, and environmental factors in moral development. The social learning perspective is also sensitive to the influences of television and other media on moral and religious development.

III. *Psychoanalysis and Religious Education*

A number of important works have appeared in the psychoanalytic tradition that can be helpful for religious educators. Gillespie has studied the phenomenon of religious conversion utilizing both psychoanalytic theory and individual psychology.[18] In this work there is a creative use of Erikson's theory and a demonstration of its usefulness in understanding the phenomenon of religious conversion. Conn has treated the same area in a broader interdisciplinary study that includes theology and developmental theory.[19]

The subject of conversion as a transforming moment has received a profound treatment in James Loder's work.[20] Drawing on many sources including his own clinical experience, Loder has brilliantly described the intellectual and affective components of transforming experiences. Loder sees a central tendency for a climatic transformation in middle years. His view is that early experiences of God have influence at this time. Loder's suggestions for ethical education emphasize value conflicts, balancing authorities, and qualities that foster creative behavior. These qualities include an emphasis on complexity rather than on simplicity, a sustainment of the tension between the rational and the imaginative, and the acceptance of personal and group differences.

Ana-Marie Rizzutto's work on the development of the idea of God in persons can serve to sensitize religious educators to the importance of parental influences on the God image.[21] Rizzutto shows how God images formed early in life through identification with parents and internalization of their values remain throughout life. From a religious perspective the adult life of religious persons can be described as the developing, revising, and negotiating of one's images of God. Rizzutto suggests that religious educators might well retrace the evolution of their God representations for this might enhance the understanding of experiences of children they teach.[22]

The influence of Ernest Becker's work has not yet been felt among religious educators although some theologians have begun to take serious account of this work.[23] Becker's life work was to build a synthesis among psychology, cultural anthropology, and theology. He came to this task from the perspective of psychoanalysis and attempted to redefine the basic image of the person as a finite individual attempting to deny and confront "creatureliness" and mortality. Though Becker wrote on education, his radical existential approach remained outside the maintream of educational theory.[24]

Though many do not find Becker's dark and somewhat Stoic view of the human condition appealing and persuasive, he presents a strong challenge to overly optimistic perspectives on human potential. His creative use of Tillich and Kierkegaard in developing a synthesis of science and religion should recommend him to religious educators. His criticisms of institutionalized forms of religion help to make educators aware of the potential of institutions for developing and fostering pathological religious attitudes and behaviors.

Psychoanalytic theory has showing great interest in family dynamics. Vergote has studied these dynamics for their moral and religious significance.[25] His research has indicated the importance of parental figures for the development of a strong moral and religious ego ideal. Vergote stresses the importance of education by parents. For him parents are deeply involved in the formation of the ego ideal in their children, which is the most important factor in education. This ego ideal is more affective than rational; its development depends greatly on parental figures.

Also, Godin has presented us with a profound treatment of the psychological dynamics of religious experience.[26] Utilizing a basically psychoanalytic perspective, Vergote points out the functional uses of religious experiences as well as their dysfunctions. Following Freud he examines the element of illusion and magic which can be found in religious experiences. The work shows both the potential and the possible dangers in religious experiences at the personal, interpersonal, and sociopolitical levels.

IV. Developmental Theories

In the past decade most religious educators have looked to developmental psychologists for insights into the theory and practice of religious education. Though this tendency has been criticized by Moran,[27] it would appear that this trend will continue. Because these theories focus on the

157

potential of persons and usually indicate stages of development, they provide for religious educators both instructural objectives and evaluative criteria for their work.

Goldman's Theory of Religious Thinking. Although Goldman has not published research on religious thinking since his original work, his work has spurred research by other scholars. Greer in a comprehensive review of research in psychology of religion in religious education has covered the debate over Goldman's basic contentions.[28] While some researchers support Goldman's thesis, others have found little justification for the Piagetian basis for religious thinking. Researchers have begun to question the abandonment of the Bible-oriented religious education which Goldman's research appeared to support. They contend that myth and symbol can be grasped validly and creatively at a concrete level.

Kohlberg's Cognitive Developmentalism. In the past decade criticisms have been leveled against the Kohlberg theory of moral development. It has been criticized for centering too exclusively on the virtue of justice and ignoring other important moral virtues. Kohlberg's definition of morality is considered by many to be culturally biased towards North American liberal culture. Carol Gilligan has pointed out that Kohlberg drew on an exclusively male sample thus causing him to define stages in a masculine manner which stresses rights and justice over responsibility, care, and love.[29] The theory has been criticized for its exaggeration of the role of reason at the expense of affect, personality, habit, and expectations of consequences. Kohlberg has also received criticism from theologians and religious educators. These criticisms have focussed on the appropriateness of his rational and juridic approach for a religiously based moral education.[30]

Kohlberg has often responded to his critics and has modified his basic theory. Stage six is now recognized more as a theoretical ideal than as a generally achievable stage. Kohlberg has also revised his understanding of stage four to give it a more positive meaning. In his latest writings Kohlberg presents evidence that his work does not contain the sexist bias that Gilligan alleges.[31]

Despite all the criticisms, one cannot toll the death knell for moral stage theory. The basic insight of the theory remains true: there is a general movement in moral development from heteronomy to autonomy. Though the function of moral reasoning may be exaggerated in the theory, one cannot deny its importance in moral development. Though justice may not be the only virtue in the moral domain, it is certainly a central one, especially in the public sphere. The least that can be said for the theory is that it provides a typology of ways in which persons engage in moral reasoning. While persons go through stages in early development, once they attain a certain degree of maturity and experience, they appear to base their moral reasoning on a number of different modes that correspond loosely to Kohlberg's stages. What determines the form of reasoning may be factors of personality, affect, habit, and expectation of consequences.[32]

Faith Development Theory. A great amount of writing has been generated by Fowler's theory of faith development which is presented in chapter 8. Sharon Parks has used the theory to provide an understanding of young adult faith as the search for meaning and identity.[33] Her work, which is somewhat limited in its almost exclusive focus on college youth, provides an important addition to the faith development literature. In an edited work, Dykstra and Parks present a full scale analysis of the theory, including Fowler's most recent restatement together with critical and constructive essays which attempt to demonstrate how the theory can be used in ministry settings.[34] Chamberlin supplies useful reflections on how the theory can be utilized by church ministers in their dealings with particular groups in congregrations.[35]

A major research work on faith development, under the direction of Kenneth Stokes, is now completed.[36] This study incorporated both survey and interview research to examine various hypotheses on faith development focusing on such variables as gender, pattern, transition periods, involvement in organized religion, involvement in social issues and concerns, presence of cognitive or affective struggles, and involvement in educational experiences. Though methodological weaknesses have been pointed out,[37] the study offers many useful suggestions for religious educators.

V. The Psychology of Women

One of the most important occurrences in the past decade has been the emergence of a feminist critique of psychology with the development of a psychology of women. Miller broke new ground with a theory which has taken women's experience seriously.[38] Gilligan's critique of the Kohlberg research has already been noted. Gilligan's work also includes criticisms of psychoanalytic theories. The most fruitful part of her work is the sketching of a morality of care and responsibility.[39] Distinctive women's ways of knowing have also been researched.[40]

Though the challenge from feminist psychologists has been mainly at the theoretical level, the finding also affect the task of religious education. Moral education needs to be attentive to the limitations of a justice ethic and the possibilities of a care ethic. Curricula should be examined to determine whether account is taken of women's experience. The use of Scriptures, church teachings, and the tradition must be sensitive to the historical contexts and understandings where these developed and the prejudices they contained.

160

References

1. John Dunne. *The Way of All the Earth*. Notre Dame, Ind.: Univ. of Notre Dame Press, 1976; *Reasons of the Heart*. Notre Dame, Ind.: Notre Dame Press, 1978.
2. Ira Progoff. *The Practice of Process Meditation*. New York: Dialogue House, 1980.
3. Bernard Spilka, Ralph Hood, and Richard Gorsuch. *The Psychology of Religion*. Englewood Cliffs, N.J.: Prentice-Hall, 1985.
4. Margaret Gorman, ed. *Psychology and Religion: A Reader*. New York: Paulist, 1985.
5. Christiane Brusselmans, Convener. *Toward Moral and Religious Maturity*. Morristown, N.J.: Silver Burdett, 1980.
6. John Elias. *Philosophical Foundations of Adult Education*. Malabar, Fla.: Krieger Publishing Co., 1980.
7. John Elias. *Foundations and Practice of Adult Education*. Malabar, Fla.: Krieger Publishing Co., 1982.
8. Gabriel Moran. *Religious Education Development*. Minneapolis: Winston, 1983.
9. Miller, Donald. "The Developmental Approach to Christian Education", in Jack Seymour and Donald Miller. *Contemporary Approaches to Christian Education*. Nashville, Tenn.: Abingdon, 1982.
10. Thomas Gromme. *Christian Religious Education*. San Francisco: Harper and Row, 1980.
11. Kenneth Barker. *Religious Education, Catechesis, and Freedom*. Birmingham, Ala.: Religious Education Press, 1981.
12. Michael Grimmitt. *Religious Education and Human Development*. London: McCrimmons, 1987.
13. John Elias, *Moral Education: Secular and Religious*. Malabar, Fla.: Krieger Publishing Co., 1989.
14. Albert Bandura, *Social Learning Theory*. Englewood Cliffs, N.J.: Prentice-Hall, 1977.

15. James M. Lee. *The Content of Religious Education.* Birmingham, Ala.: Religious Education Press, 1986.

16. Robert Sears, et al. "How Conscience Develops." In C. E. Nelson, ed. *Conscience: Theological and Psychological Perspectives.* New York: Paulist, 1973.

17. Albert Bandura, op. cit.; J. P. Rushton. *Altruism, Socialization and Society.* Englewood Cliffs: Prentice-Hall, 1980.

18. V. Bailey Gillespie. *Religious Conversion and Personal Identity.* Birmingham, Ala.: Religious Education Press, 1979.

19. Walter Conn. *Conversion.* Birmingham, Ala.: Religious Education Press, 1980.

20. James Loder. *The Transforming Moment.* San Francisco: Harper and Row, 1981.

21. Ana-Maria Rizzutto. *The Birth of the Living God.* Chicago: University of Chicago Press, 1979.

22. Ana-Maria Rizzutto. "The Psychological Foundations of Belief in God." In C. Brusselmans. *Toward Moral and Religious Maturity.* op. cit.

23. Ernest Becker. *The Denial of Death.* New York: Free Press, 1973; *Escape from Evil.* New York: Free Press, 1975.

24. Ernest Becker. *Beyond Alienation: A Philosophy of Education for the Crisis of Democracy.* New York: Braziller, 1967.

25. Antoine Vergote. "The Dynamics of the Family and its Social Significance for Moral and Religious Education." In C. Brusselmans, convener. *Toward Moral and Religious Maturity.* op. cit.

26. Godin, Andre. *The Psychological Dynamics of Religious Experience.* Birmingham, Ala.: Religious Education Press, 1985.

27. Gabriel Moran, op. cit.

28. John Greer. "Fifty Years of the Psychology of Reli-

gion in Religious Education," Two part article. *British Journal of Religious Education*. Vol. 6, No. 2, Spring 1984 and Vol. 7, No. 1, Autumn 1984.

29. Carol Gilligan. *In Another Voice*. Cambridge, Mass.: Harvard University Press, 1982.

30. Craig Dykstra. *Vision and Character: A Christian Alternative to Kohlberg*. N.Y.: Paulist, 1981; Stanley Hauerwas. "Character, Narrative, and Growth in Christian Faith." In C. Brusselmans, *Toward Moral and Religious Maturity.* op. cit.

31. Lawrence Kohlberg, *The Psychology of Moral Development*. San Francisco: Harper and Row, 1984.

32. John Elias, *Moral Education: Secular and Religious*. Malabar, Fla.: Krieger Publishing Co., 1989.

33. Sharon Parks, *The Critical Years: The Young Adult Search for a Faith to Live By*. San Francisco: Harper and Row, 1986.

34. Craig Dykstra and Sharon Parks, eds. *Faith Development and Fowler*. Birmingham, Ala.: Religious Education Press, 1986.

35. Gary Chamberlain. *Fostering Faith: A Minister's Guide to Faith Development*. New York: Paulist, 1988.

36. Kenneth Stokes. *Faith Development in the Adult Life Cycle*. Minneapolis, Minn.: Faith Development Life Cycle, 1987.

37. Richard Osmer. "Faith Development in the Adult Life Cycle: A Review." *Religious Education*, Vol. 84, No. 4, Fall 1989, pp. 483–493.

38. Jean Baker Miller. *Toward a Psychology of Women*. Boston: Boston Press, 1976.

39. Carol Gilligan. op. cit.

40. Mary Field Belenky et al. *Women's Ways of Knowing: The Development of Self, Voice, and Mind*. New York: Basic Books, 1986.

INDEX OF PRINCIPAL SUBJECTS